# Cake Decorating
# Made Easy

# Cake Decorating
# Made Easy

## Robyn King

# Contents

I would like to dedicate this book to my much loved family who have tolerated the many nights where I have frantically kept working to get the job done.

Also to my mother who inspired me to do something that I loved and my many friends and family who believed in my ability and encouraged me to keep going.

Thank you.

Robyn

# Introduction

My passion for baking and decorating cakes began as a child.

This love has grown over many years and continues to be what drives me every day. I love to see the delight on people's faces when the cake is presented, the reaction is very rewarding, it ranges from excitement, to laughter, speechlessness and occasionally tears (happy ones of course).

I began baking as a very young child, my family lived on a property of a few acres and creating in the kitchen was encouraged by my mother who was a very good cook herself, many valuable skills were developed and learnt whilst watching her bake for the family.

Cake decorating is very rewarding whether you are doing it as a hobby or professionally. Many enjoyable hours can pass while creating with fondant, flower paste, ganache, buttercream and the many other varieties of icing used.

I know that when I come up with a new idea or design, I can't wait to try and test techniques to achieve the look that I am after.

While there are basic techniques to follow, there are no rules to say that they have to be followed precisely, so if there is a better way or a faster way to achieve the look that you are after and it works, there is no reason why it can't be done a different way.

Keep in mind that all things used must be edible and food safety standards and outlines should be followed at all times. I have tried to make each step as simple and as clear as possible.

Often there is more than one way to do something so choose the method that you are most comfortable with to begin, and once confidence has been gained with the basics, more difficult methods and techniques will become much less of a challenge and your own creativity will drive you to try new things.

There are new tools being produced all the time which often make jobs easier or faster, however I always like to know that I can produce something that doesn't have me relying on the availability of a product, ending up with cupboards full of tools that never get used or go out of fashion quickly is something that I try to avoid.

Let the fun begin…

Happy baking!

Recipes

# Chocolate Mud Cake

## Ingredients

250 g (9 oz) unsalted butter
200 g (7 oz) dark chocolate
250 g (9 oz) caster sugar
300 ml (10 fl oz) water
175 g (6 oz) self-raising flour
25 g (1 oz) cocoa
2 eggs
1 tsp vanilla
1 tbsp coffee or rum (optional)

## Method

1.  Preheat the oven to 150°C (300°F).
2.  Line a 22 cm (9 in) round cake pan.
3.  Place the butter, chocolate, sugar and water into a saucepan and heat through until all the ingredients are combined. Leave to cool.
4.  In a mixing bowl combine the flour, cocoa powder, eggs, vanilla and rum.
5.  Once the liquid in the saucepan has cooled, pour into the bowl with the flour, cocoa powder and eggs, mix until combined.
6.  Pour into a greased, lined baking tray and bake for approximately 1½ – 2 hours depending on size of tin and height of the cake.

# White Mud Cake

## Ingredients
375 g (13 oz) white chocolate
250 g (9 oz) butter
300 ml (10 fl oz) milk
100 g (3½ oz) caster sugar
2 tsp vanilla extract
2 large eggs, beaten
125 g (4½ oz) self-raising flour
200 g (7 oz) plain flour

## Method
1. Preheat the oven to 150°C (300°F).
2. Grease a 22 cm (9 in) round cake tin and line the base and sides of the pan with baking paper.
3. Place the chocolate, butter, milk and sugar in a large saucepan, place over a low heat and stir frequently until the chocolate and butter have melted. Stir until the mixture is completely smooth.
4. Allow the mixture to cool.
5. Add the vanilla and eggs to the cooled chocolate mixture and stir until combined.
6. Combine the flours together and sift.
7. Add one cup of flour to the chocolate mixture and stir well, add the remaining flour and stir until smooth and lump free.
8. Pour the mixture into the prepared pan – the mixture will be quite runny.
9. Bake in the oven for 1 hour 20 minutes or until a skewer inserted into the cake comes out clean.
10. If the cake is browning too much, cover loosely with aluminum foil.
11. Once cooked remove from the oven, leave the cake in the tin to cool completely before tipping out.

# Carrot Cake

serves
**16**

## Ingredients

2 eggs
250 g (8 oz) caster sugar
175 ml (6 fl oz) vegetable oil
½ tsp vanilla
125 g (4 ½ oz) plain flour
1 tsp bicarbonate of soda
½ tsp mixed spice
½ tsp nutmeg
½ tsp cinnamon
1½ medium carrots
125 g (4 oz) walnuts
125 g (4 oz) shredded coconut

### Cream cheese filling

125 g (4½ oz) cream cheese
50 g (2 oz) butter
350 g (12½ oz) icing sugar
    (confectioners' sugar)
1 tsp finely grated orange rind
1 tbsp fresh orange juice

## Method

1.  Preheat the oven to 175°C (325°F).
2.  Line a 22 cm (9 in) round cake pan.
3.  Mix together the eggs, caster sugar, vegetable oil and vanilla until creamy.
4.  Sift the flour and bicarbonate of soda and add to the bowl, add the spices, carrots, walnuts and coconut, gently mix through.
5.  Place in the lined tin.
6.  Bake for 45–50 minutes.

## Method for cream cheese filling

1.  Place all ingredients into a mixing bowl and beat together until creamy.

# Boiled Christmas Cake

serves
**25**

## Ingredients

500 g (17½ oz) mixed fruit
100 g (3½ oz) glace cherries
375 g (13 oz) sugar
1 tbsp golden syrup
125 g (4½ oz) butter
1 tsp bicarbonate of soda
250 ml (8 fl oz) cold water
2 eggs
175 g (6 oz) cold cooked
    pumpkin, mashed
175 g (6 oz) plain flour
175 g (6 oz) self-raising flour

## Method

1. Preheat oven to 160°C (325°F).
2. Place in a saucepan the mixed fruit, cherries, sugar, golden syrup, butter, bicarbonate of soda and water.
3. Bring to the boil and simmer for 20 minutes.
4. Allow to cool, add the beaten eggs and mashed pumpkin.
5. Sift the flours together and add to the mixture.
6. Place mixture into a greased lined 20 cm (8 in) square cake tin and bake for 1½ – 2 hours.
7. When cooked wrap in a towel to cool.

# Fruit Cake

serves
**25**

## Ingredients

1 kg (2¼ lb) mixed fruit
300 ml (10 fl oz) sweet sherry,
   (Soak the fruit in sherry for a
   week or more)
250 g (9 oz) butter
250 g (9 oz) brown sugar
100 g (3½ oz) golden syrup
4 large eggs
375 g (13 oz) plain flour
25 g (1 oz) cocoa powder
½ tbsp mixed spice

## Method

1. Preheat the oven to 150°C (300°F).
2. Line a 22 cm (9 in) cake pan.
3. Blend together the butter and sugar (don't aerate the mixture).
4. Add the golden syrup, then add the eggs one at a time.
5. Sift the flour and cocoa powder and add to the other ingredients in the bowl.
6. Add the mixed spice.
7. Blend together with the fruit mixture which has been soaking in the sherry.
8. Place the batter into the cake tin.
9. Bake in the oven for 2½ hours, it may take longer for larger cakes.

# Sultana Cake

serves **16**

## Ingredients
500 g (17½ oz) sultanas
250 g (9 oz) butter
250 g (9 oz) caster sugar
1 tsp grated lemon rind
½ tsp lemon essence
1 tsp vanilla essence
3 eggs
350 g (12½ oz) plain flour
75 g (3 oz) self-raising flour
3 tbsp milk
50 g (2 oz) mixed peel

## Method
1. Preheat the oven to 180°C (350°F).
2. Place the sultanas into a saucepan and add sufficient cold water to just cover them. Bring to the boil and lower the heat, simmer for five minutes.
3. Drain and rinse under cold water then drain in a colander until cool.
4. Cream together the butter, sugar, lemon rind and essences until light and fluffy, then add the eggs one at a time.
5. Add the sifted flours, and when thoroughly mixed stir in 3 tablespoons of milk. Add the well drained sultanas and peel and mix through.
6. Place into a lined 22 cm (9 in) tin and bake in the moderate oven for 1 hour, then reduce the temperature to 160°C (325°F) and bake for a further 45–60 minutes.
7. Cool in the tin on a wire rack.

# Madeira Cake

## Ingredients

250 g (9 oz) butter
500 g (16 oz) caster sugar
2 tsp vanilla essence
½ tsp lemon essence
6 eggs
350 g (12½ oz) plain flour
½ tsp salt
250 g (9 oz) light sour cream

### Crumble topping

45 g (2 oz) plain flour
1 tsp of cinnamon
¼ tsp nutmeg
2 tsp sugar
1 tsp butter

## Method

1. Preheat oven to 160°C (325°F).
2. Cream together the butter, sugar, vanilla and lemon essence until light and fluffy.
3. Add the eggs one at a time beating well between each addition.
4. Add the flour and salt to the mixture alternating with the sour cream and mix until just combined.
5. Place in a deep, lined 20 cm (8 in) square cake tin. Sprinkle with the crumble topping if the cake is not being iced with fondant.
6. Bake for 2–2¼ hours until cooked through.

## Method for crumble topping

1. Mix together the flour, cinnamon, nutmeg and sugar.
2. Rub through the butter with your finger tips until the mixture resembles breadcrumbs.

# Egg and Dairy-Free Chocolate Cake

serves
**16**

## Ingredients

450 g (16 oz) self-raising flour
75 g (3 oz) cocoa
500 g (17½ oz) caster sugar
½ tsp salt
500 ml (16 fl oz) water
150 ml (5 fl oz) vegetable oil
60 ml (2 fl oz) lemon juice
1 tsp vanilla essence

## Method

1. Preheat the oven to 180°C (350°F).
2. Sift the flour and cocoa powder together, place into a large mixing bowl with the caster sugar and salt.
3. Add the water, oil, lemon juice and vanilla, combine well.
4. Pour the mixture into a greased and lined 22 cm (9 in) cake tin.
5. Bake for 1½ – 2 hours until cooked through.

# Gluten-Free Mud Cake

serves
**16**

## Ingredients

250 g (9 oz) dark chocolate,
   grated
250 g (9 oz) almond meal
250 g (9 oz) sugar, raw
1 tbsp gluten-free baking powder
1 tbsp cocoa
150 g (5 oz) butter
6 eggs

## Method

1. Preheat oven to 180°C (350°F).
2. Grease and line a 22 cm (9 in) cake pan.
3. Mix together the almond meal and grated chocolate.
4. Place the sugar, baking powder and cocoa into a food processor.
5. Add the butter and eggs and mix until combined.
6. Bake at 180°C (350°F) for 20 minutes and then reduce the heat to 160°C (325°F) for a further 60 minutes, or until cooked through.
7. Leave in the tin for 15 minutes then turn out onto a wire rack to cool.

# Red Velvet Cake

serves
**16**

## Ingredients

300 g (10½ oz) white sugar
250 ml (8 fl oz) vegetable oil
2 eggs
50 g (1½ fl oz) red food coloring
1 tsp white vinegar
250 ml (8 fl oz) buttermilk
1 tsp bicarbonate of soda
350 g (12½ oz) self-raising flour
35 g (1½ oz) cocoa powder
1 tsp vanilla essence

## Icing

225 g (8 oz) cream cheese,
    softened
125 g (4½ oz) butter, softened
500 g (17½ oz) icing sugar
    (confectioners' sugar)
1 tsp vanilla essence
60 g (2½ oz) chopped pecans
30 g (1 ¼ oz) whole pecans

## Method

1. Preheat the oven to 175°C (350°F).
2. Line three 20 cm (8 in) round pans with baking paper.
3. In a large bowl, mix together the sugar, oil and eggs.
4. Add the food coloring and vinegar to buttermilk.
5. Add the bicarbonate of soda to the flour and cocoa powder.
6. Add the flour mixture and buttermilk mixtures alternately into the sugar mixture.
7. Mix well. Stir 1 teaspoon of vanilla into the batter.
8. Pour the batter into the prepared pans.
9. Bake for 20–25 minutes, or until done. Remove from the oven, and cool on wire racks.

## Method for the icing

1. Mix together the cream cheese, butter, icing sugar and vanilla. Stir in the chopped nuts.
2. Spread the icing over the cooled cake and sandwich the layers together. Decorate with the whole pecans.

# Ganache

makes
**900g**

## Ingredients

300 ml (10 fl oz) single cream
600 g (21 oz) dark chocolate

## Method

1. Chop the chocolate into small pieces and place in a mixing bowl.
2. In a saucepan bring the cream to the boil.
3. Pour the cream over the chocolate, mixing with a wooden spoon until all the chocolate has melted.
4. Allow the ganache to cool before using.
5. Ganache can be used as is or it can be mixed gently with a beater until it is at spreadable consistency (don't over mix as the mixture will curdle).

Note: Ganache is a chocolate and cream mixture used to spread between cake layers and to cover and seal cakes in preparation for fondant to cover the cake. It can be made with dark chocolate, milk chocolate or white chocolate, the amount of chocolate used varies accordingly, the method for all varieties remains the same.

» To make dark chocolate ganache the ratio of cream to chocolate is 1:2, 1 part single cream to 2 parts dark chocolate.
» For milk chocolate ganache the ratio of cream to chocolate is 1:2.5, 1 part single cream to 2.5 parts milk chocolate.
» To make white chocolate ganache it is 1:3, 1 part single cream to 3 parts white chocolate.

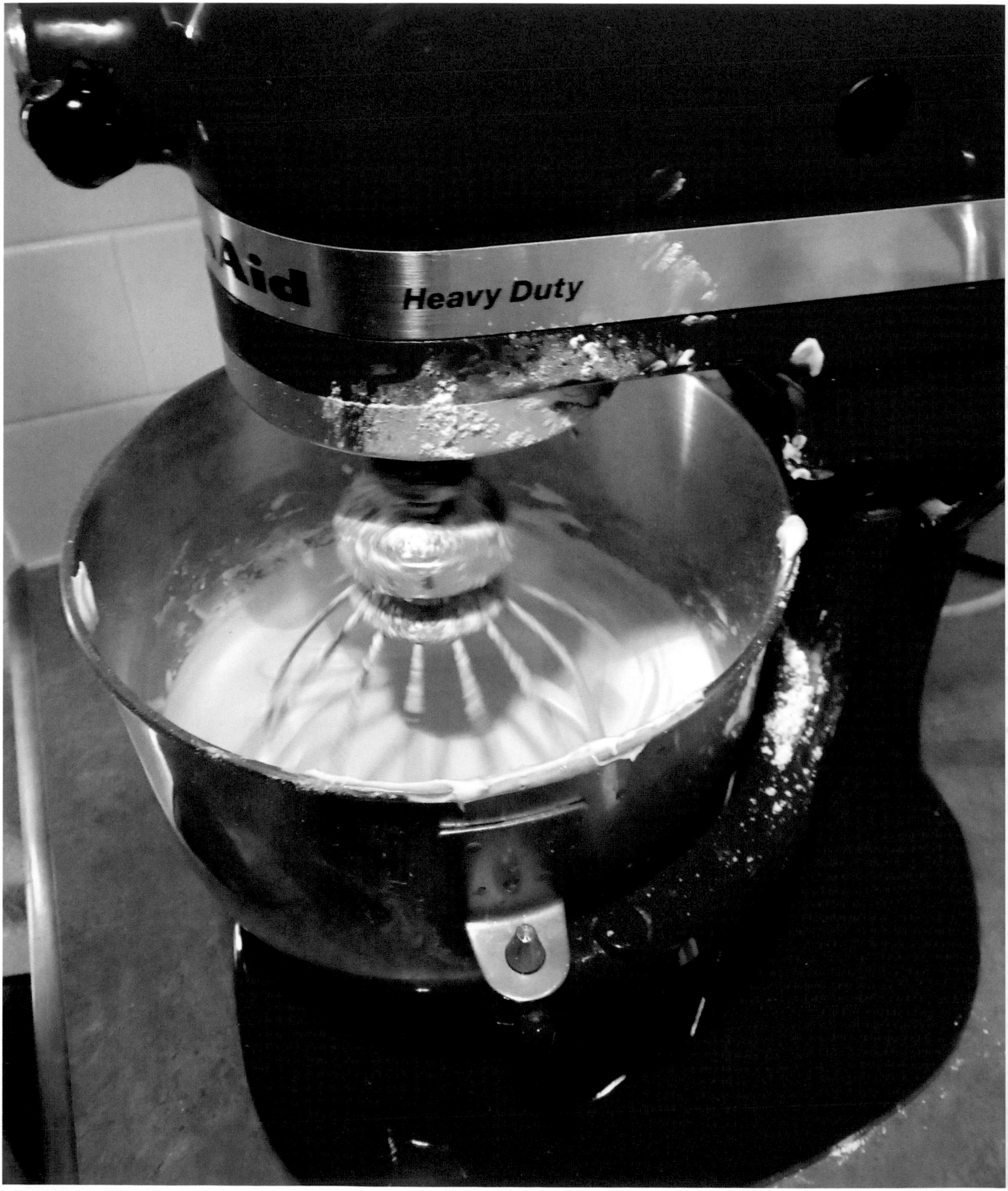
Heavy Duty

# Royal Icing

makes
**500g**

## Ingredients

3 egg whites (egg white powder
can be substituted for
fresh egg – make up as per
manufacturer's instructions
then continue with recipe)

600 g (21 oz) pure icing sugar
(confectioners' sugar), sifted
(not all of it may be used)

1 tsp lemon juice (or 4 drops
acetic acid)

## Method

1. Place the egg whites in a large bowl. Add some of the sifted icing sugar to the mixture and mix in a food processor on low speed.
2. Keep adding the icing sugar a little at a time. Once half the icing sugar is added, put in the lemon juice or acid. Keep adding the icing sugar slowly. When the mixture looks like thick whipped cream and forms soft peaks, it is ready for piping.

Note: Keep royal icing covered at all times with a damp cloth or in an airtight container as the icing crusts quickly which causes lumps. Royal icing is used for flood work, extension work, lace work, shell work borders, holding together flowers or sticking flowers to cakes.

## Method for 'run in' icing

1. To make run in icing for flood work or making plaques, take some royal icing, place into a small bowl and mix with water, a few drops at the time. Continue this until the icing is thick enough to flood without being too thin. It should be smooth when piped, with no lumps to be seen.

Note: Mixing with the water can cause air bubbles in the icing, so it is always good to cover the icing and let it rest for 30 minutes after adding the water. Once the bubbles have come to the surface give it a slow stir to break the air bubbles, then continue to place the icing in piping bag to pipe.

# Buttercream Icing Using Vegetable Shortening

makes
**1.5kg**

## Ingredients

250 g (9 oz) vegetable shortening

1 kg (2¼ lb) pure icing sugar
   (confectioners' sugar)

125 ml (4 fl oz) warm water

½ tsp vanilla essence

## Method

1. Place the vegetable shortening in a mixing bowl and beat for one minute to precondition.
2. Gradually add the icing sugar and mix well between additions.
3. Add water as needed until the desired consistency is achieved.
4. The icing should be light and fluffy.
5. Add vanilla to taste.

   Note: Any flavorings or colors can be added to the mixture. Icing can be made to any quantity using a 1:4 ratio, 1 part shortening to 4 parts icing sugar.

# Gum Paste (Flower Paste)

makes
**500 g**

## Ingredients
60 ml (2 fl oz) cold water
2 tsp gelatine
½ tsp liquid glucose
½ tsp white vegetable fat
600 g (21 oz) icing sugar
    (confectioners' sugar)
½ tsp CMC (tylose)

## Method
1.  Using a small saucepan, place the gelatine in the cold water and
    soak for a few minutes until clear.
2.  Put the pan on the stove and warm through while stirring.
3.  Just before it boils take the mixture off the heat and add the
    liquid glucose and white fat.
4.  Begin to add the sifted icing sugar, be sure to stir well before
    adding more so that it goes white. Once the mixture comes
    together and is too hard to mix in the pot, place some icing sugar
    on the work bench and begin to knead in enough icing sugar to
    make a very soft dough, at this point the CMC can be added.
5.  Wrap the mixture in plastic and put in an airtight container. The
    paste will firm up overnight and will be ready to use the next day.
    Adjust the consistency using more icing sugar if the paste is still
    too soft.

# Sugar Syrup

makes
**500 ml**

### Ingredients
250 g (8 oz) sugar
250 ml (9 fl oz) water

### Method
1.  Place the sugar and water in a saucepan.
2.  Bring to the boil and simmer for a few minutes.
3.  Allow to cool.

Note: Larger or smaller amounts of syrup can be made by using equal amounts by weight of sugar and water.

Sugar syrup can be stored in the refrigerator for up to a week.

Sugar syrup is used for many things. It can be brushed onto the layers of the cake before ganache is spread through, to prevent the cake from going dry during the decorating process.

Syrup can also be lightly brushed over the ganached cake before fondant is placed on top to help the icing stick to the surface. It can also be used as a form of glue to help fondant cut outs to stick to the fondant iced cake.

# Preparation and Tools

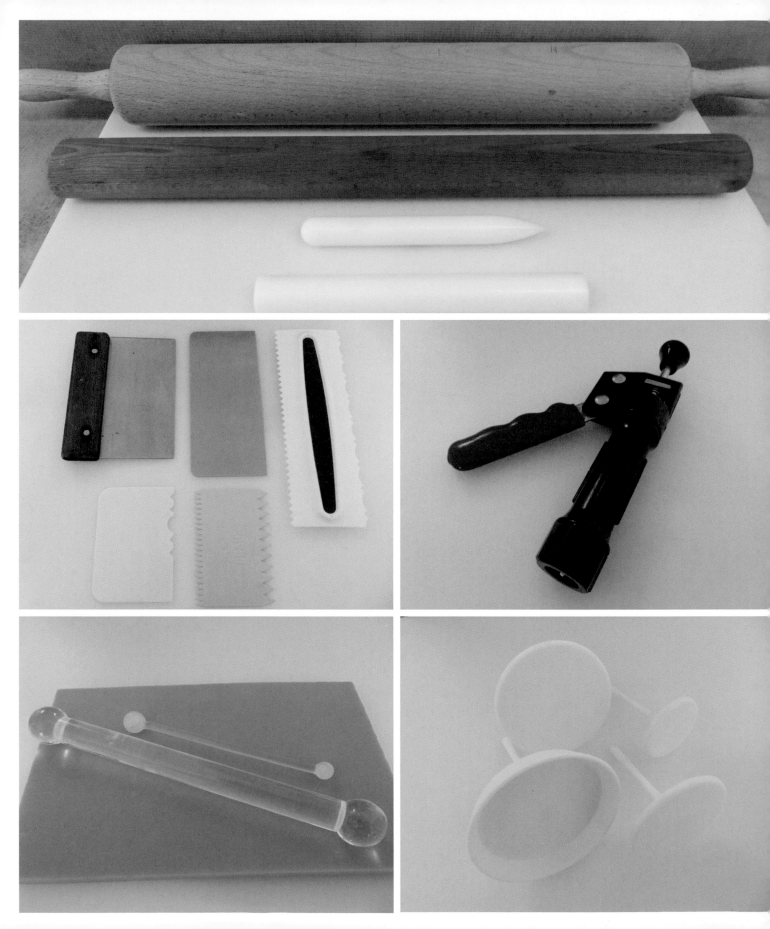

# Preparation and Tools

## Basic tools

- Rolling pin
- Icing smoothers
- Cornflour
- Palette knife
- Sharp knife
- Scissors

## What you will need when preparing to ice and decorate a cake

- Cake or cakes depending on how many tiers
- Fondant for covering the cake
- Base boards the same sizes as the cakes for ganaching
- Larger board to present the cake on
- Straws or wooden dowels for support if tiered
- Royal icing to adhere the cake to the board
- Flowers or decorations which can be made in advance
- Ribbon or lace
- Wooden rolling pins – used to roll fondant when covering a cake
- Silicon rolling pins – used to roll icing when making flowers or cutting out small pieces of fondant
- Metal scrapers – to wipe away excess cream or ganache from the sides of a cake
- Plastic scrapers – makes patterns in the icing when scraping around the side of the cake with either ganache, cream or icing
- Clay gun or extruder – used to extrude thin icing strips

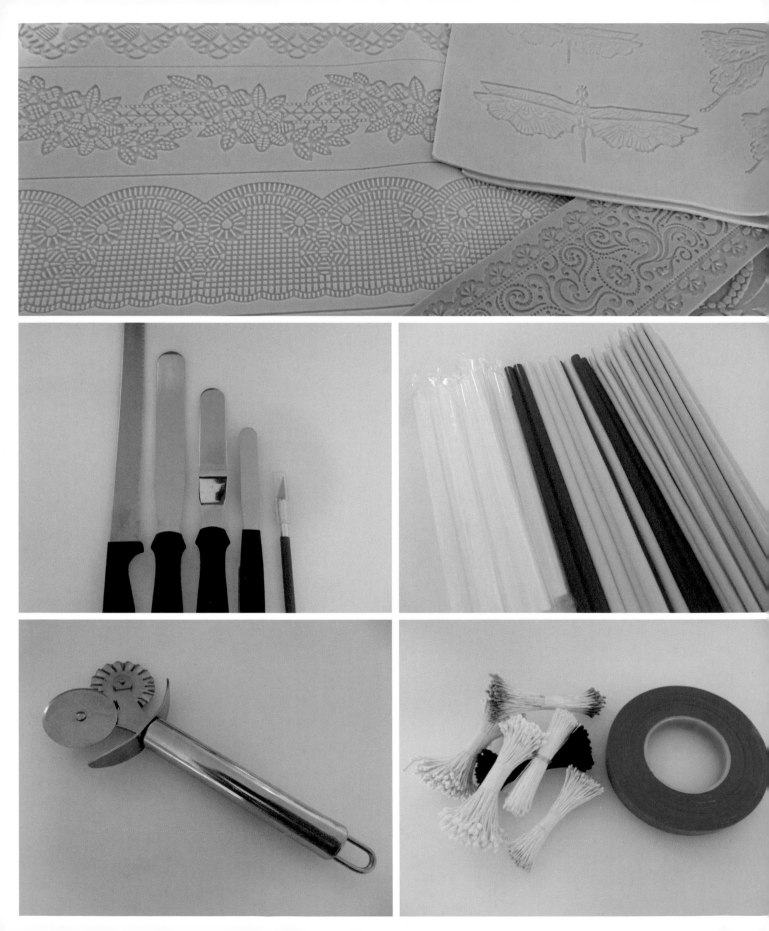

- Balling tools and petal pad – to smooth the edges of petals and ruffles. Also used to push indentations into petals and smaller flowers
- Flower nails and flat heads – used to pipe buttercream flowers
- Silicon lace mats – for making cake lace
- Knives – saw knife, three sizes of palette knives, scalpel
- Roller cutter – used when cutting ribbon strips or straight edges
- Stamens and flower tape – for making centers in flowers

# Lining a cake tin

Care should be taken when preparing the cake tin. The cake itself is the foundation for your masterpiece so it should be lined accurately.

When lining a square tin the corners should remain sharp to ensure that the finished product still looks like a square and not a square with round corners. When baking cakes that take a long time in the oven, such as fruit cake or mud cake, lining the tin with three or more layers of paper will help prevent a dark crust forming on the outside.

1. Measure the circumference of the tin and cut a length of paper that will easily go right around the inside of the tin, overlapping slightly.
2. Fold the paper over to create layers, leaving 2.5 cm (1 in) to fold up at the base. Once the fold line has been made take a pair of scissors and make cuts in the paper up to the fold mark.
3. Neatly place the paper inside the tin, with the cut pieces sitting on the bottom of the tin.
4. Using the tin as a template trace around the base and a cut out pieces of paper that fit neatly inside the tin. Place on top of the cut pieces inside the tin, this will hold the side paper in place.

NOTE: Cooking spray can be sprayed in the tin first to help the paper stay in place.

Techniques

# Preparing the Cake Using Ganache

The ganache on the outside of the cake is something that needs particular attention. This step ensures a smooth and straight base for your fondant to be applied to.

Take care and time when applying the ganache as the end result will depend hugely on the accuracy of the ganaching process.

Once the cake has been baked, it should be cooled completely before cutting and ganaching. Once the cake is cool, place in the fridge for half an hour or so, this gives a firmness which makes the cake easier to handle.

1. Trim the top of the cake so that it is flat and level then turn cake over so that the base becomes the top of the cake. The height of the cake will vary depending on the design. If layers of cream or ganache are going inside, cut the cake horizontally as many times as desired, place the base layer onto a base board.
2. Soften the ganache by mixing or slightly warming it, so that the ganache spreads smoothly without creating holes in the cake or dragging crumbs through the ganache. Spread a thin layer of ganache in between the layers of cake and restack the layers to form the original shape of the cake.
3. Spread a thin coating of ganache all over the outside of the cake, keeping it as smooth as possible, refrigerate for a further five minutes. Once the first layer has firmed a second coating can be applied.
4. Take a scraper that is at least as high as the cake and holding it at a 90° angle to the cake press against the base board and smooth the outside edge. Tidy up the top edge of the cake with a pallet knife and continue to level and smooth until the sides and top are perfectly covered with the ganache.
5. Allow the cake to set overnight. The ganache firms up on standing which makes the cake more stable for the fondant to be applied. The cake is now ready to ice!

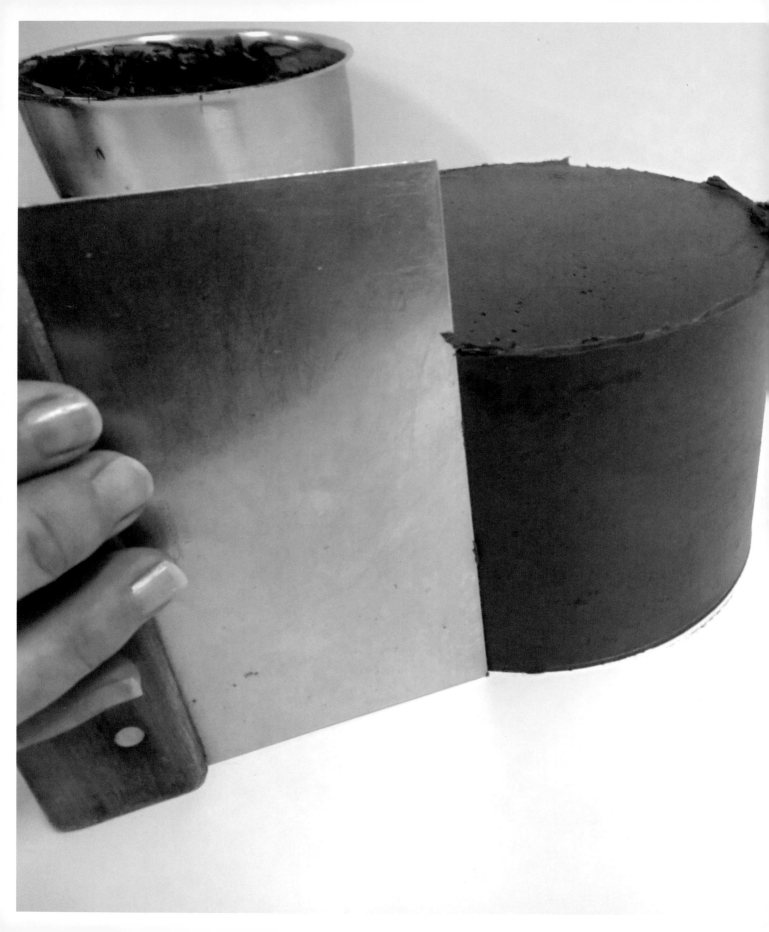

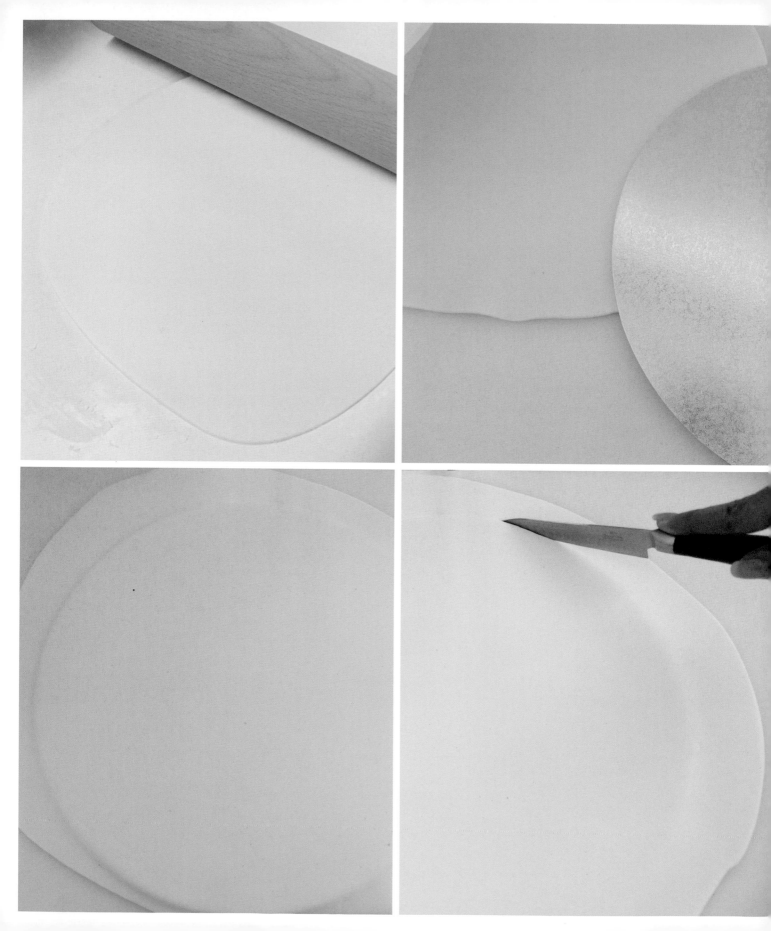

# Covering the Board

The board is the presentation tray for the finished product.

Just as much care should be given to icing the board as is given when icing the cake itself.

The size of the board will depend on your cake design. I like to use a board which is 7.5–10 cm (3–4 in) bigger than the actual size of the cake, this gives a 3.8–5 cm (1½–2 in) clearance around the cake.

Sometimes it will be necessary to use a larger board if there is to be writing or ornaments on the board.

1. Roll ready-to-roll (RTR) icing to 2–3 mm (0.07–0.1 in) thick.
2. Spray or brush water onto the top surface of the board to make the icing stick.
3. Pick up the icing and lay it over the board, smooth with an icing smoother to ensure that there are no air bubbles under the icing.
4. Using a flat blade knife (not too sharp as it will damage the foil) trim the excess icing from the edge of the board.
5. Spread a thin layer of royal icing in the center of the board so that the cake, when placed in position, will stay in place and not slide around on the board.

   NOTE: It is best to ice boards well in advance so that the icing has time to dry, it is thus less likely to get damaged when placing the cake on the iced surface.

# Covering Cakes with Ready-To-Roll (Fondant) Icing

Covering a cake with fondant takes practice. The smooth surface of the cake indicates the quality of the finished product.

It is essential that the fondant be kneaded well before rolling out and placing on the cake, this gives elasticity to the fondant and makes it less likely to crack.

Much care should also be given when smoothing the fondant over the cake, finger marks are easily left on the surface which leaves a messy, unprofessional look to the cake.

'RTR icing' 'fondant' and 'plastic icing' are all the same type of icing but it is often referred to using these different names. Ready-to-roll (RTR) icing is a smooth, formal icing used to cover traditional and modern style cakes.

Prepare the cake with ganache as previously described. Once the ganache has set (overnight is best) the cake can be iced. Prepare the surface of the ganached cake by brushing a very light covering of sugar syrup over the cake.

Precondition the RTR by kneading it well before beginning to roll out, this makes the icing pliable and less likely to crack.

Measure the cake from the base of one side to the other, to determine the size that the icing needs to be, there should be excess icing in order to be able to trim back without folds developing in the icing.

1. Begin to roll out the icing using a light dusting of cornflour to prevent the RTR from sticking to the bench. Be sure to roll evenly, and move the icing regularly by giving half turns, this will prevent ridges from forming on the edge. Gradually roll the RTR to 3–4mm (0.1–0.15 in) in thickness.
2. Placing both hands under the rolled icing gently pick up the RTR and place directly over the prepared cake.
3. Work quickly to first smooth the top and gently press the icing onto the top edge of the cake and then work down the sides.
4. Once the icing is stuck to the surface begin to smooth with plastic smoothers. Rub the entire surface until there are no bumps or air bubbles.
   NOTE: Air bubbles can be removed by piercing the icing with a fine pin to let the air escape, then continue to smooth the icing (take care and responsibility when using a pin to burst bubbles as something so tiny and sharp can easily be misplaced and lost in the icing).
5. Trim any excess away with a sharp knife, if the trimmings are free from crumbs the leftover icing can be reused on the next cake or board.

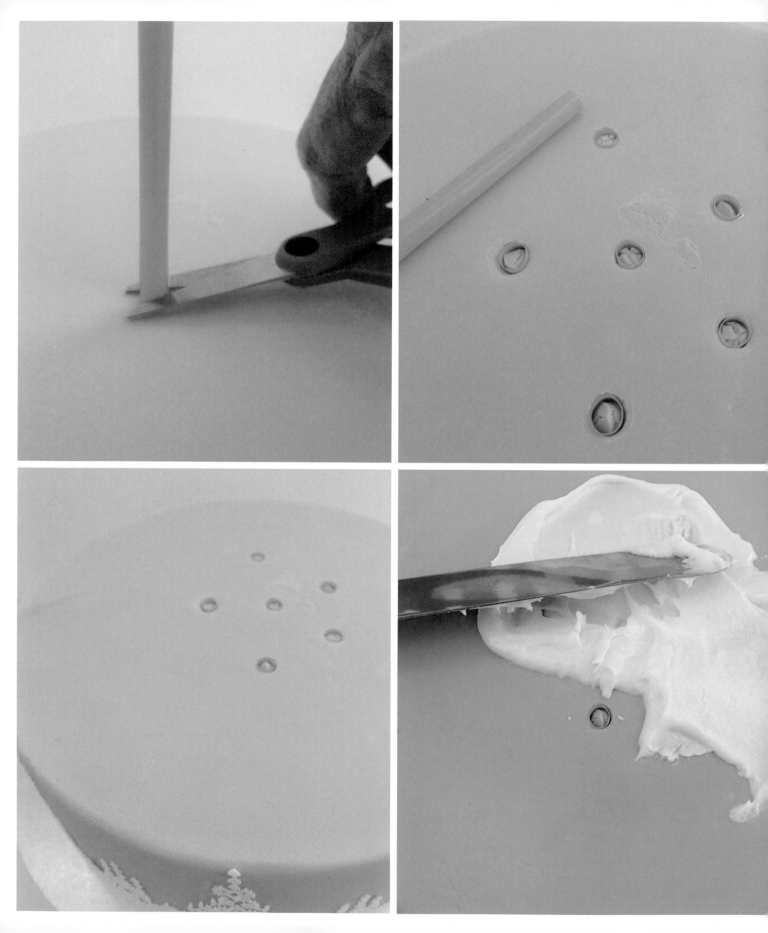

# Stacking Cakes

Stacking cakes on top of each other gives a grand appearance to your cake design.

Cakes are surprisingly heavy especially once they are iced with fondant, so supports are needed to prevent the cakes from sinking into each other and collapsing.

Each cake is individually iced and should be on a board of its own, this gives the bottom of the supports something to sit on which prevents the layers from collapsing.

The larger the cake the more supports will be needed to take the weight of the cakes on top.

Soft cakes such as sponge cakes are not strong enough to support both the fondant and tiers on top, the use of soft cakes should be avoided.

1. First place the base cake onto the base board using some royal icing to secure.
2. Using large tea straws or wooden dowels push the straw into the middle of the base cake and mark the straw with a pencil at the top of the cake. Cut the excess from the top of the straw and repeat with remaining straws. Cut each straw the same height to ensure that the next cake sits evenly on top of the other. The amount of straws used is determined by the size of the cake sitting on top. When stacking three tiers the amount of straws would be approximately six for the base cake, five for the middle and four for the top tier.
3. Once the straws have all been inserted into the cake spread some royal icing on top of cakes and stack each cake on top of each other.
4. The base board of each cake should be sitting on top of the straws with royal icing in between.

# Piping Techniques

Piping is a skill that needs to be practiced in order to perfect the art.

There are many different types of tubes (piping tips) available. The most commonly used tips are the small round tips size 1–2 and the shell work tips 5–8.

The larger tips are used for buttercream style softer icing and they are tips 1M and 2D, these are used to pipe rosettes and look fabulous on cupcakes.

Begin with a practice board and a round icing tip.

When using royal icing keep it covered to prevent it from forming a crust which in turn will cause blockages in the icing tube

1.  Start by filling the piping bag with royal icing, place the tube close to the work surface so that it connects, then lift and move the tube while keeping even pressure on the bag. Continue to pipe lines until they are straight.
2.  Next hold the bag with the icing tip close to the surface, draw curved lines in order to gain control of the bag. Once you are comfortable with this try writing. I find that a nice flowing style is not too hard to achieve once even pressure is maintained.
3.  A small star tube, number 5 or 8, is also a good place to start when piping shell work. To practice this fill a piping bag with royal icing and pipe small balls and drag the tip downwards while releasing pressure off the bag.
4.  Practice piping in straight lines or around the edge of a cake pan until the piped shell work is even and straight. Practice is the key to becoming an expert piper.

# Naked Cakes

The most recent trend in cake decorating is the soft iced, lighter style cakes.

There are many types of icing and cream which can be used on such cakes. Some examples are:

- Swiss meringue buttercream
- Italian meringue buttercream
- Fresh cream
- Buttercream
- Mock cream
- Soft icing
- Ganache
- Cream cheese icing

Naked Cakes, sometimes referred to as semi-naked cakes, are simplistic yet elegant.

The cakes are usually layered with the filling exposed. They can be dusted in icing sugar (confectioners' sugar) or they can have a thinly spread icing or cream on the outside, exposing the outside edge of the cake.

A slightly more formal look is to ganache the cake using a straight edge scraper to achieve a very clean, defined look but still have some of the cake showing through.

This style of cake looks especially beautiful with fresh flowers or fresh fruit to decorate. Care must be taken when using fresh flowers as some flower varieties are poisonous. The stems should never come into contact with the cake, they can be placed into a cake spike and then be pushed into the cake.

1. Bake cakes of your choice and leave to cool.
2. Pipe cream or filling of your choice between the layers and stack on top of each other. The cakes can be decorated with flowers at this point or more cream can be spread around the edge.
3. To mask the sides of the cake with cream simply spread the cream roughly on the sides of the cake then using a scraper or straight edged pallet knife smooth the sides, pushing against the cake so as that the crust is exposed slightly.

   NOTE: The same process is used to spread the ganache. This will give a more defined edge as the ganache is more stable therefore it is easier to achieve sharp straight edges.

Caramel or a dessert style sauce can also be drizzled over the edge of the cake, this looks great when using fruit to decorate the top of the cake.

# Piping with Buttercream

Piping ruffles and textures on the sides of cakes has also become a popular alternative to RTR or fondant iced cakes.

While the formal looking smoothness of fondant is a great surface to work on many people find that the heavy fondant icing is not something that they like to eat. Buttercream is a great alternative in such instances.

There are some wonderful piping tips on the market which produce the most elegant ruffles using buttercream or soft icing.

A stable icing is a must, anything that is too soft or has a low melting point could pose a problem, especially when using some of the thicker style piping tips.

Consideration should also be given to transportation of the finished article.

1.  Prepare the cake by leveling the top and layering using the same preparation method as if icing a fondant iced cake.
2.  Mask the sides and top of the cake with whatever icing you choose to use. When piping ruffles or any kind of pattern that is piped in a straight line it is helpful to score the icing with a comb style scraper, so that there is a line to follow which will make it easier to achieve straight piping.
3.  Place the cake on a turntable to make the piping process flow easier.

    STYLE A:
    *   Using a number 070 tube (ruffle tube) pipe along the bottom of the cake following the marked lines around the side. Pipe one row at a time then move up and follow a line which raises the ruffle half way up the previously piped ruffle.
    *   Continue to the top of the cake.

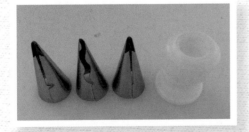  

## STYLE B:

- Using the number 126 tube (Rose Petal Tube), hold the bag filled with icing so that the fat end of the tube is at the top and the fine edge is at the bottom. Start at the base of the cake, keeping constant pressure on the piping bag, turn the cake slowly around using the turntable. Moving up the cake continue to pipe more rows following the lines marked on the cake to get a straight finish. Continue to do this until you have piped all the way up the side of the cake.

STYLE C:

- Using a ruffle tube number 87, pipe vertically up the side of the cake moving the tube from side to side (about 1 cm (0.3 in)) and moving up the cake at the same time. Continue piping around the cake, keeping the ruffles vertically straight and even.

## STYLE D:

- Using a plain round tube, pipe teardrop style bulbs around the cake horizontally. This can be done ombre style going from dark to light or vice versa all the way up the cake.
- Start by piping a bulb then release the pressure from the bag and drag the tip away from the bulb.

 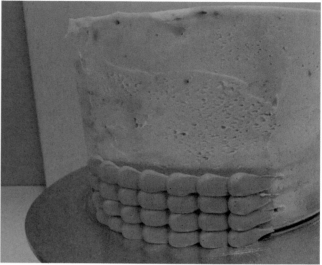

## STYLE F:

- Using a plain round tube, pipe graduating colors around the cake (ombre style). With a straight edged scraper smooth the sides so as that the colors merge leaving a flat surface.

  NOTE: The scraper can be immersed in hot water to give a smoother finish.

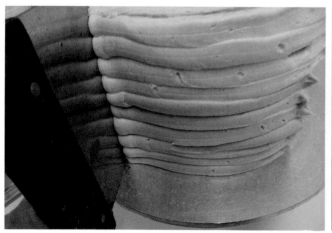 

## STYLE E:

- Using a large star tube (1M or 2D are the most common), pipe rosettes around the cake. This can also be done ombre style.
- To make a rose with this tube start in the center, bring the piping bag up a little and continue to pipe once around. Repeat this process for every rosette until the cake is fully covered.

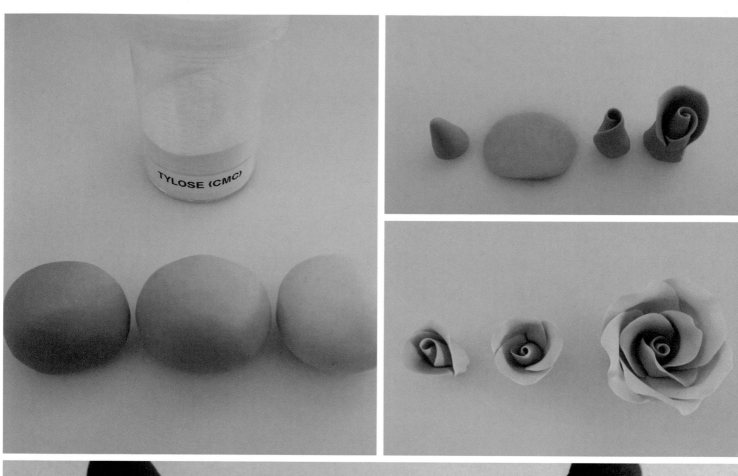

# Hand Molded Roses

Roses on a cake, whether it be for a formal occasion such as a wedding or a simple birthday cake, always looks stunning.

There are so many varieties of roses, some have very ruffled petals, some are tight and very rounded, they can have a lot of petals or fewer petals but they all look beautiful.

Roses when made from icing don't need to be botanically correct, they simply need to resemble a rose, so keep it simple when starting out, once a basic rose is achieved expand on technique once you become comfortable with the process.

To make a simple rose using fondant, tylose or CMC needs to be added to make the flower set firm. Flower molding paste or gum paste can also be used.

Color the icing with food coloring, liquid color, paste or gel color can be used. Make three different shades of the desired color.

1. Starting with the darkest colored icing first, make a cone shape which is about 1 cm (0.3 in) across the base.
2. Take another piece of dark icing, start by rolling it into a ball then flatten it between the forefinger and thumb. Rub the top edge of the petal to make it paper thin (use cornflour on fingers to prevent sticking).
3. Place the cone in the middle of the petal and wrap the petal around the cone forming a point at the top.
4. Using a 1 cm (0.3 in) round piece of the second darkest shade, roll another ball and flatten it. Rub the top edge to make it thin. Using water and a paint brush, dampen the base of the petal and stick it to the side of the rose center. Shape the top edge to give the petal movement. Repeat this two more times so that there are three petals around the bud.
5. Continue making five more petals in the same way using the lighter shade of icing.
6. Carefully pinch off the excess at the base of the rose and leave to dry.

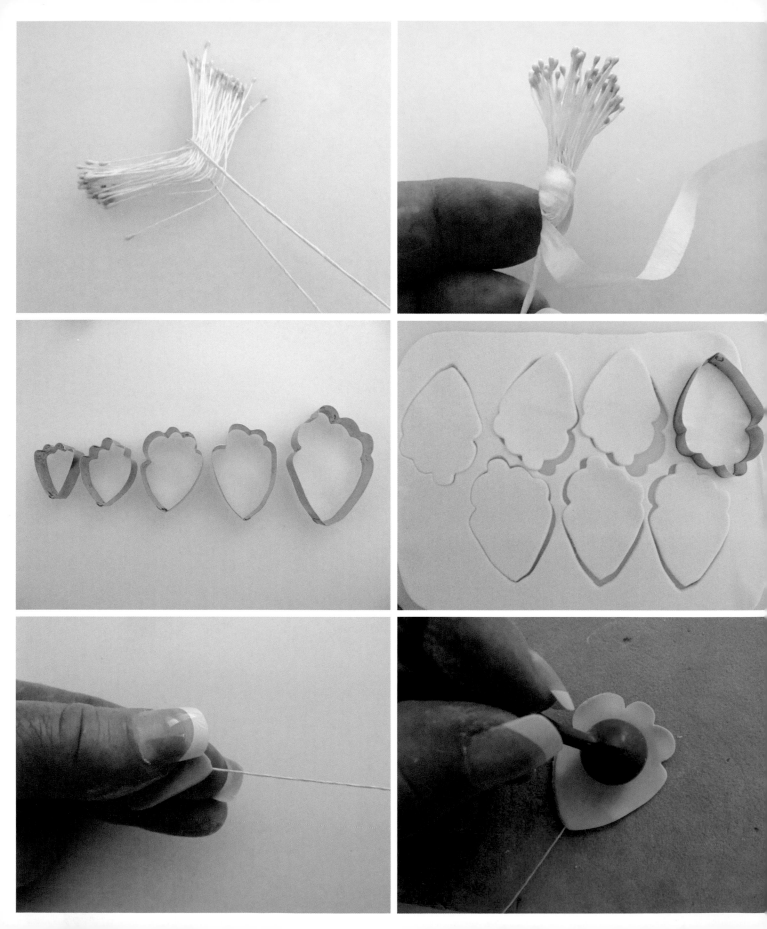

# Large Peony Rose

The peony rose is a beautiful, elegant alternative to a spray of flowers.

There are many varieties of peony roses to chose from but the similarity in all varieties are the mass of petals which makes up each flower.

The peony is a stand alone flower, with its large petals and shear elegance there is no need to use too many flowers on a cake, one single flower on the top of a tiered cake is enough.

Each flower has at least 25 petals to make a large peony, I often have many more than that as the peony looks especially beautiful if it is full of petals.

The center of the flower can have stamens or it can be made without, a more closed center with small petals looks lovely too, sometimes I make a fantasy style peony with a center dipped in cachous or white hundreds and thousands.

1. Stamens are often used in wired flowers and are readily available at good cake decorating stores. Take a generous bunch of stamens in the color of your choice, bend in the middle, using 24 gauge wire secure the bunch. Wrap florist tape around the base to hold the stamens and wire together.
2. Using gum paste, color the paste with food coloring or leave it white, roll the icing to 1 mm (0.03 in) thickness leaving the back end of each petal slightly thicker so as that a wire can be inserted.
3. Using a set of five petal peony cutters, cut out petals. Starting from smallest to largest cut three smallest, then four of the next size up, then five, six, and finally seven of the largest petals.
4. Dampen the end of the wire with water and insert into the thicker end of the petal, using a balling tool and petal pad smooth the fine end of each petal and push a curve into the middle of each. Set in a curved tray to dry. Drying time is at least 24 hours (drying times vary depending on weather conditions and the type of gum paste used).
5. Once the petals have dried arrange them around the stamens starting from the smallest, secure with florist tape and continue layering the petals until the largest ones are used.

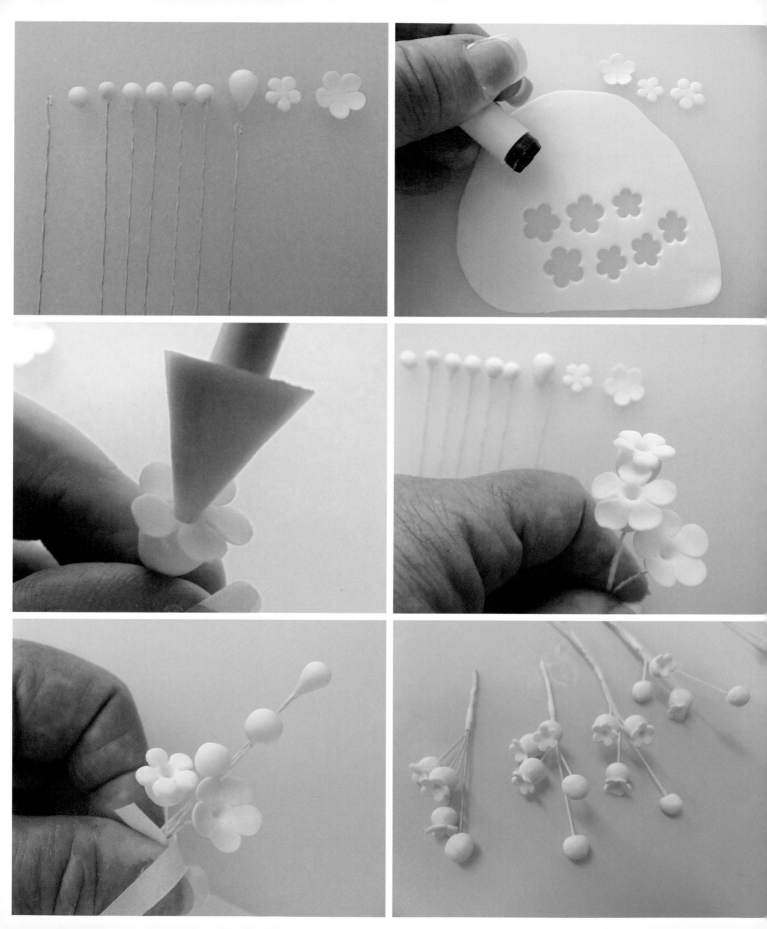

# Small Filler Flowers

Tiny flowers are always time consuming to make so they have become less popular than they once were.

The snowflake (sometimes called snowdrop) is the one I like to make as a fantasy style flower as it is quicker than making a realistic flower yet it still looks dainty and elegant.

The main use for these tiny flowers is to fill gaps between larger flowers and to give the cake a soft and delicate and very pretty look.

1. Roll small balls of gum paste (baby pea size) and secure to a fine wire (26 gauge).
2. Roll out some more gum paste very thinly (almost transparent) using a small blossom cutter cut out tiny flowers. Using flower glue or a mixture of tylose and water stick the cut out blossom to the top of the ball.
3. Leave some balls plain without the blossom on top to resemble little buds, bunch three to five together and secure with florist tape to make small sprays of flowers.
4. Green spots can be painted on the tips to resemble the real flowers.

# Simple Flowers Using RTR

Simple flowers using cutters are an effective way to decorate both cupcakes and larger cakes.

They can be simply cut out and stuck flat onto a cake or they can be cut out and pressed with a balling tool on petal pad to soften the edges to give a more realistic look to the flower.

Flowers can be made well in advance, once dry they can be stored in a cardboard box away from humid areas.

> NOTE: Save the silica gel sachets which is often found in packaging. Keep a sachet in the box with flowers to absorb any humidity that may be in the air. Be sure not to let it come into contact with the edible flowers.

1. Take some RTR and knead a good pinch of tylose (CMC) to 100 g (3.5 oz) RTR.
2. Roll the icing to 1 mm (0.03 in) thickness, push flower cutters into the icing then place them onto a petal pad.
3. Push on the outside of the petals to shape and make the edges thin and realistic.
4. Leave to dry. Larger flowers may need some support while drying – a curved cake pan can be used or flower formers can be purchased from specialty cake stores.

Happy
80th Birthday
Meg

# Piped Buttercream Flowers

Hand piped flowers are becoming increasingly popular. To transform buttercream into a beautiful flower in seconds is something that still excites me, it happens so fast and looks incredibly pretty.

To cover a whole cake with flowers made from sugar paste or fondant would be a very long process, so the buttercream alternative is definitely a method to try as it is so much faster yet looks very professional if executed neatly.

To pipe flowers, either royal icing or buttercream can be used. Whatever the choice of icing may be, a firm consistency is needed.

## Rose

1.  Place a small piece of waxed paper or baking paper on the flat end of a flower nail.
2.  Using a rose petal piping tip and piping bag filled with icing, pipe a ball of icing in the center of a flower piping tool. Hold the piping bag so the tip is vertical, keeping the thinnest part of the tip at the top and the thicker part to the bottom.
3.  Next pipe one petal by piping in an arched formation.
4.  Start the next petal in the middle of the first.
5.  Repeat this process for as many times as needed until you reach the size of the rose required.
6.  Remove the paper with the flower on top and leave to dry, flowers can also be placed in the refrigerator to firm so they can easily be placed onto a cake without damaging the petals.

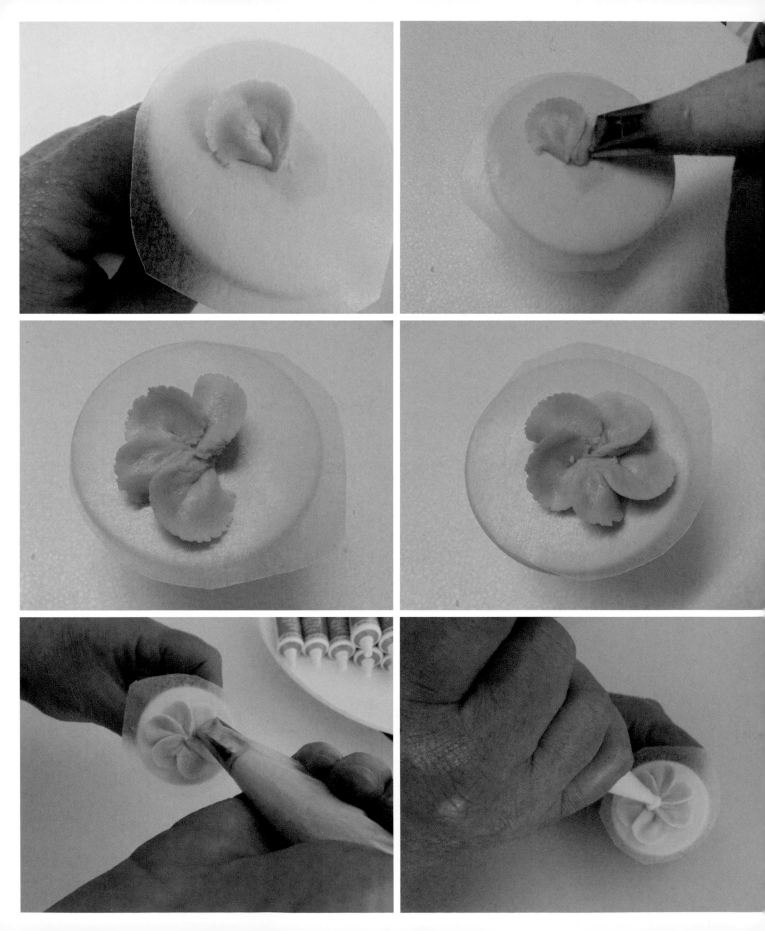

# Daisy

1. Use the flat end of a flower nail and a rose petal tip. Secure a small piece of waxed paper to the surface of the disk with a small amount of icing.
2. Starting in the middle of the disk with the thinnest part at the top, pipe long arches, extending from the center, out to the edge and back.
3. To do this, put pressure on the bag until an arch is formed and release pressure as the icing is pulled back towards the center of the disk.
4. Repeat until petals have been piped all around.
5. A second layer can be piped on top to make a double daisy.
6. Using a small round tube pipe dots in the middle to make the center using a different color.
7. Remove the paper from the flat surface of the nail tool and repeat to make more daisies.
8. Leave to dry or refrigerate.

# Lettering Using Cutters

Letter cutters give a professional look to any cake with wording either on the cake or on the board. There are many different sizes available from very large cookie style cutters down to tiny elegant cutters. Take a close look at the depth of the cutter before rolling the fondant, this will give a clear indication of how thin the fondant needs to be rolled. If the letters are getting stuck in the cutter it is usually because the fondant hasn't been rolled thin enough and is becoming jammed inside the cutter.

1. Add a small amount of tylose to the RTR.
2. Roll out the fondant so as that it is almost transparent, less than 1 mm (0.03 in) thick.
3. The cutters are usually quite shallow, if the icing is too think the letters will get stuck in the cutter.
4. Use cornflour to prevent sticking. Press the cutter down on the rolled fondant, then give it a shake to make sure it has cut right through.
5. Lift the cutter, tap it on the table and the letters should fall out quite easily.
6. Allow the letters to harden then adhere to the cake or the board with some royal icing or sugar glue.

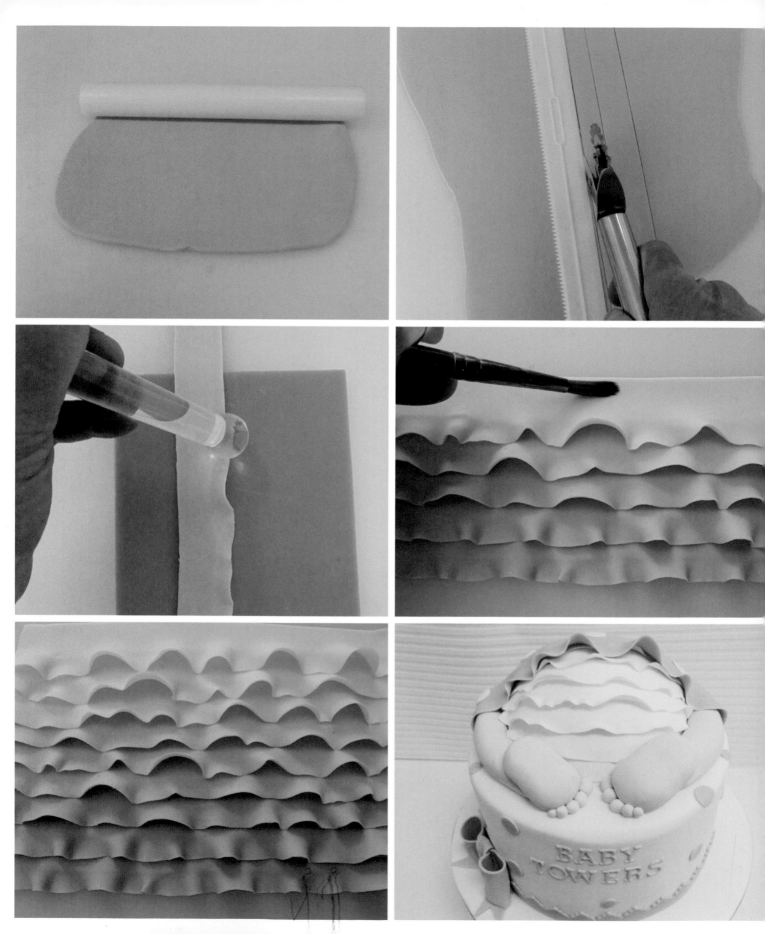

# Fondant Ruffles

There are many styles of ruffles that can be used to decorate cakes.

Some ruffles are made using long lengths of fondant that can be placed around the cake in rows while others can be made from small pieces of icing and placed on the cake side-by-side.

Ruffles can be facing downwards which means the first row is placed at the base of the cake, continue placing the ruffles on until they reach the top of the cake.

Ruffles can be placed facing upwards as well, so start at the top and continue down the sides of the cake.

Cover the cake with a thinner layer of fondant than is usually used to avoid the finished cake from becoming too heavily covered with icing. This gives the ruffles a good surface to stick to. Any bumps that may show through from the icing being too thin will be covered up by the ruffles.

1. Knead some tylose into the RTR for strength. (A good pinch of tylose per 100 g (3.5 oz) of RTR is ideal.)
2. Roll out long strips of RTR to 1 mm (0.03 in) thickness, with a pizza cutter or strip cutter, cut lengths of icing that are about 2.5 cm (1 in) wide.
3. Place the strip onto a petal pad and use a balling tool press on one side, the icing should curl and be wavy.
4. Dampen the straight side with some water and place onto the iced cake.
5. Continue around the whole cake, start the next row halfway up the first to cover the edge and continue until the whole cake is covered.

# Bows and Ribbons

Bows placed on top of a cake look gorgeous for any celebration. They can be bright and vibrant or soft and pretty depending on the occasion.

Bows can either sit upright on top of a cake, or on the side.

RTR with tylose can be used to make firm setting loops, however, to be sure that any humidity doesn't effect the finished product I prefer to use gum paste.

## Bow

1. Roll out the icing to 1 mm (0.03 in) thickness.
2. With a scalpel or sharp knife cut two curved shapes to make the bow using one piece of icing.
3. Dampen the middle of the bow shape and fold the ends in to meet in the middle, gently push down with the end of a paint brush or icing tool.
4. Cut another straight strip of icing to go around the middle and secure with sugar glue or water.
5. Cut two more pieces for the ends of the bow and secure them to look as if they are coming out from underneath the bow.
6. Use royal icing to secure to either the top or the side of the cake.
   NOTE: When making a large bow tissue can be place inside the rounded part of the bow to stop it from collapsing, remove once the bow has dried.

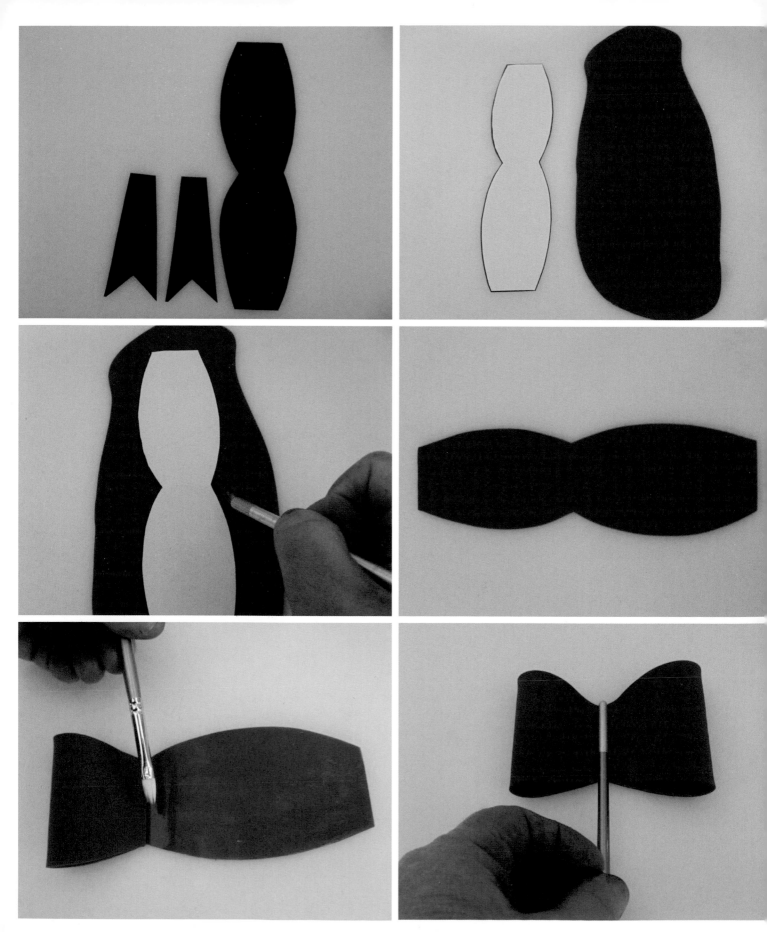

# Looped Puffy Bow

1. Roll out RTR to 1mm (0.03 in) thickness.
2. Cut strips with a strip cutter or a pizza style roller cutter to about 1cm (0.4 inch) width and 8 cm (3 in) length (these sizes can vary depending on the size of the cake). At least 24 loops will be needed however this can vary depending on how big the bow needs to be.
3. Fold each strip to form a loop and secure with sugar glue at the base.
4. Cut a point at the base to make the bows easy to insert into the cake once dry.
5. Make some pieces that are not looped for the ends.
6. Leave to dry overnight.
7. Once dry arrange in a dome shape starting at the base and adding as many loops as needed to form a dome, royal icing is need to secure the points in the center.

# Brush Embroidery

Brush embroidery has made a comeback, using a paintbrush has turned cakes into a canvas with royal icing and food coloring as the new medium.

The texture that brush embroidery gives to the surface is unique, making the finished product very much a piece of artwork.

Once the embroidery has been brushed onto the surface of the cake, small piping details can be added to give another dimension to the work

1. To begin, prepare the cake with fondant and leave for 24 hours so that the working surface becomes firm.
2. Fill a piping bag with some royal icing using a number 2 icing tip.
3. Pipe the outline of a petal, pipe only one petal at a time as the royal icing needs to remain soft.
4. Using a small paintbrush, dip the brush in water (not to much, you may need to wipe some of the water off to prevent pooling).
5. Using the paintbrush, drag the icing towards the center of the flower with the wet brush so as that the edges are thicker and the center thins out.
6. Continue doing the same with each petal until the flower is complete.
7. Leaves can be done in the same way, the veins can be added by dragging a toothpick through the icing to make a line down the center.

# Fondant Iced Cupcakes

Fondant iced cupcakes are a beautiful alternative to the usual rosette piped on top of the regular shop bought cupcakes.

If time taken to produce the perfect cupcake is no barrier, then the sky is the limit.

Less is often more, however there is so much decorating that can be done on a humble cupcake. When working with fondant on a cupcake many different finishes can be applied.

A few examples are:
- Stenciling
- Air brushing
- Impression patterns
- Cake lace
- Piped decoration
- Hand molded roses
- Cut-out designs

## METHOD

1. Cover cupcakes with a small amount of ganache or buttercream, this will also fill any uneven spots on the cupcake.
2. Roll some RTR to 2 mm (0.08 in) thickness.
3. Use a round cutter slightly larger than the cupcake as it has to fit over the slight hump on the cake.
4. If the icing is to have an impression pushed into it press the pattern on before placing the icing on the cake.
5. Place the cut out circle on top of the cupcake.
6. Use a small ball of RTR to rub over the top of the cupcake to smooth the surface.
7. Decorate the cupcakes with pre-made bows or flowers or any other decoration that you choose to make.

# Booties and Shoes

Making booties or shoes to go on top of a child's cake or christening cake can be made using molds, cutters or a template.

Once the base shape has been cut from fondant the process for putting the shoe together is the same, simply join the pieces together with sugar glue then decorating with trim and shoe laces or buttons.

Ballet shoes are also achieved by using the same process, a different pattern is used to cut out the pieces but is similarly put together. I like to spray ballet shoes and booties with pearl shimmer to give the shoes a satin finish which makes them look realistic.

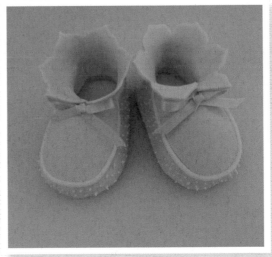

# To Make Booties Using a Template or Cutter

## METHOD

1. Knead some RTR which has tylose added (½ teaspoon for 100 g (3.5 oz) of RTR fondant).
2. Roll out to 1 mm (0.03 in) thickness and cut the base of the shoe first.
3. Cut the front part of the bootie and dampen the edge of the sole with sugar glue to stick them together. A small ball of icing may need to be placed inside for support until dry.
4. Cut out the back part of the bootie and using some more sugar glue stick the back onto the sole and shape around to meet the front of the bootie.
5. Roll out some more RTR in a contrasting color and cut strips to place around the base of the bootie.
6. Use a clay gun/extruder to pipe tubular shoe laces and trim the top edge of the bootie with a slightly thicker tube also from the extruder.

Templates for booties and ballet slippers

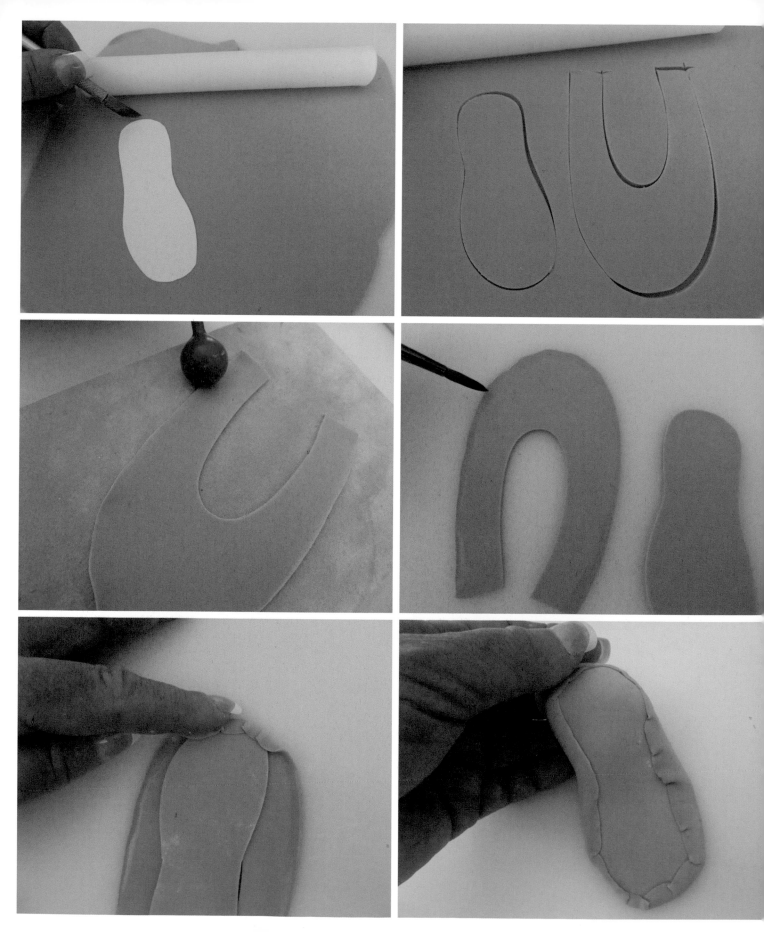

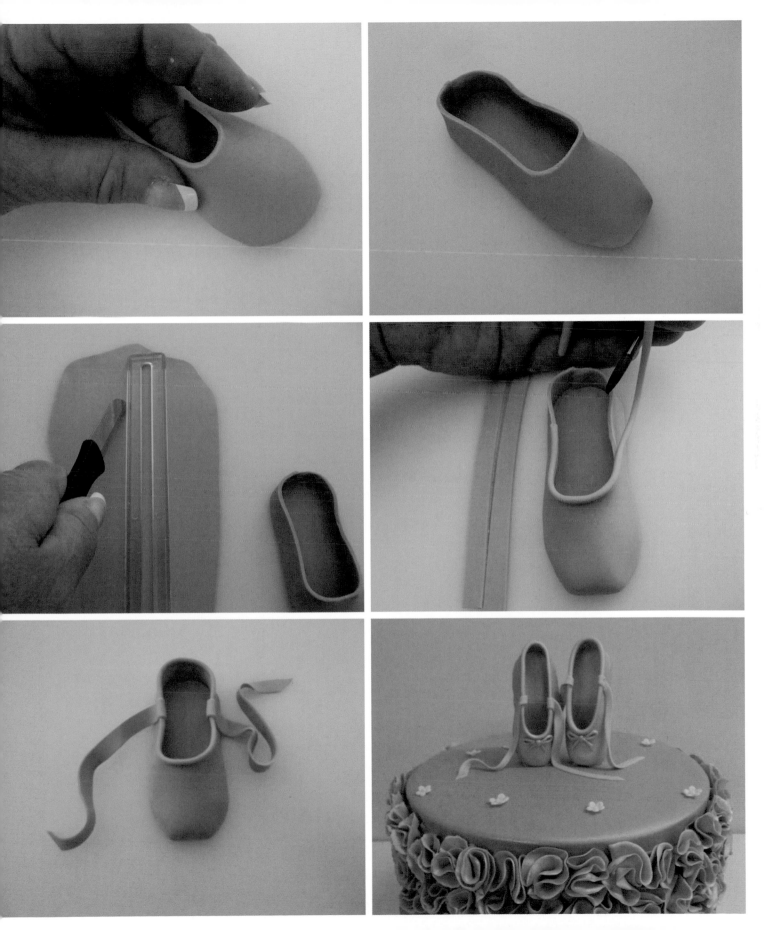

# 2D Pictures

Creating your own design from cut out pieces of fondant is much less time consuming than making 3D figures.

The pieces can be put together without the need for drying time.

The finished decoration sits flat on the surface of the cake which also means that transportation of the cake is less risky as the pieces cant be bumped off the cake.

2D cutouts also look wonderful around the sides of the cake which means the board can also be used to further enhance the design.

Items such as rocks, fences or reeds can be placed over the top to bring the characters to life.

## METHOD

1. Cake decorations can be tailored to match the theme of an event, invitations are often a good place to start.
2. Using a picture, card or print, trace or draw a template of the object that is required and cut it out with a pair of scissors.
3. Segment the picture into pieces where there are different colors or where a join needs to be accentuated.
4. Roll out RTR in the colors that are needed and cut out the pieces.
5. Starting with the larger base pieces, arrange them directly on the cake or on a plaque, then continue to add smaller detailed pieces until finished.
6. Some parts may lend themselves to rolling to give a rounded edge instead of a clean cut edge.
   NOTE: A clay extruder is a handy tool to use for this as fine even strips can be pushed through to make hair, grass, boarders etc.

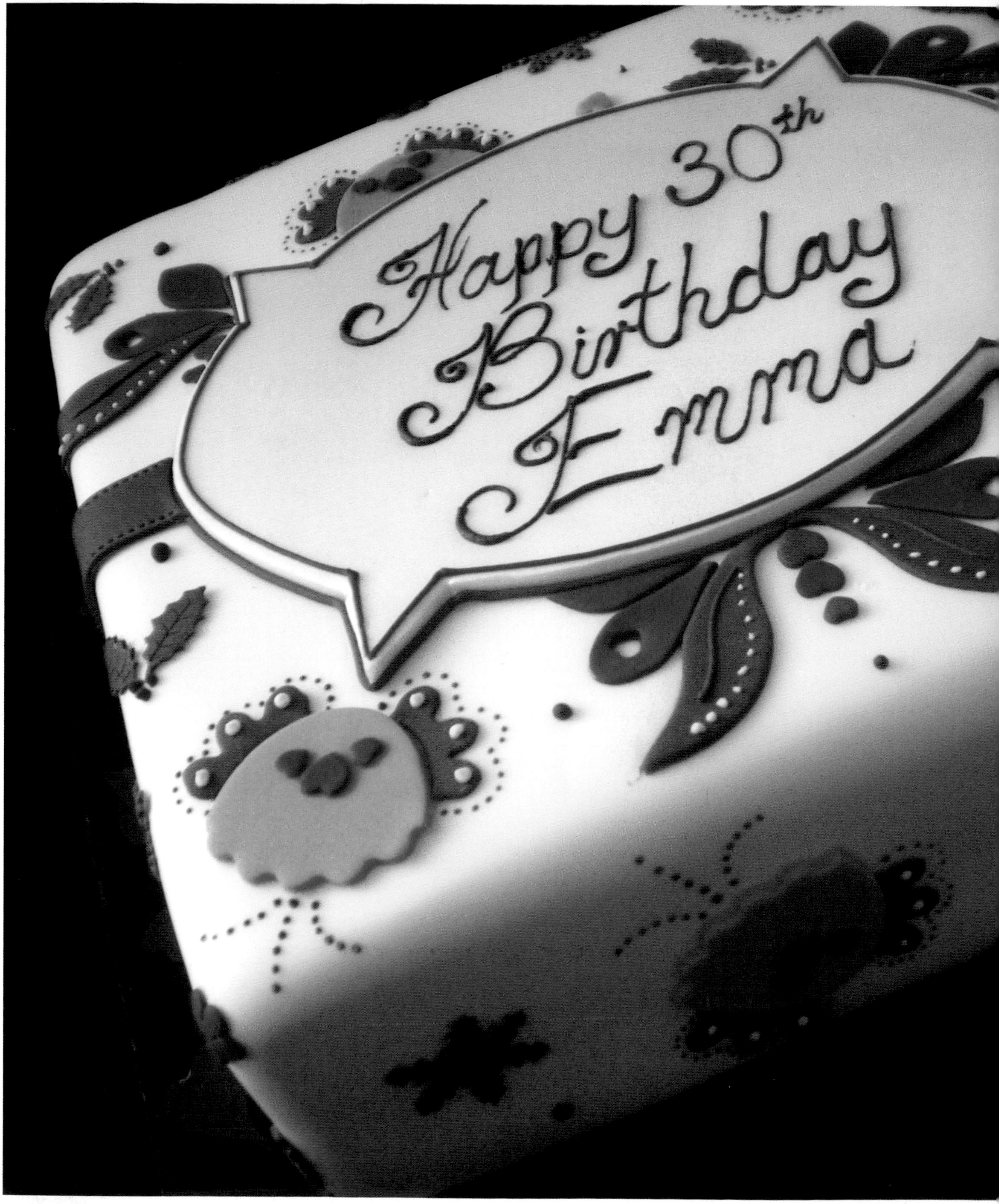
Happy 30th
Birthday
Emma

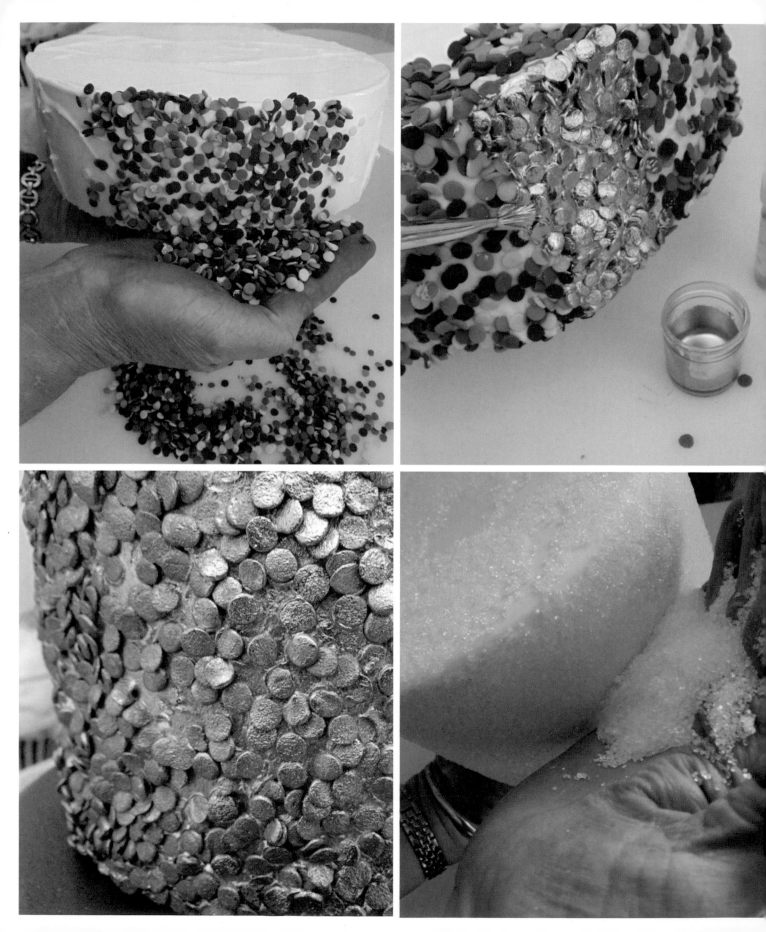

# Sequins

Sequins on the side of a cake which have been painted in gold or silver is quite a new trend in cake design. It is very eye catching and glamorous, especially on wedding cakes.

Sequins can be purchased in specialty cake stores. They are usually brightly colored.

Other textures that could also be used in place of the sequins are:
- Sanding sugar
- Hundreds and thousands
- Cake sprinkles
- Silver or gold cachous or sixlets

## METHOD

1. Ice the cake of choice in thinner than usual RTR icing (2 mm (0.08 in)) and leave to set firm.
2. Using a soft peak royal icing mix, spread royal icing all over the cake surface.
3. Picking up handfuls of sequins, press them securely into the royal icing until the cake is totally covered and leave to dry.
4. Use a mixture of gold dusting powder and rose spirit or alcohol to form a paint. With a thick brush paint the luster all over the sequins to give a good coverage and leave to dry. A second coat maybe needed if the sequins are still showing color through the gold.

# Cake Lace

Cake lace is a fairly new and a popular form of embellishment for cakes, especially for wedding cakes. There are many brands of cake lace available, all of which are easy to use, be sure to follow the manufacturers instructions as the procedure varies depending on which brand you are using.

Once the lace is mixed, spread the mixture into a silicon lace mold, these can usually be placed in the oven on a very low heat to hasten the drying process – always check the manufacturers notes for drying instructions and drying time.

Note: When spreading the lace into the mold, take care to fill every tiny groove with the mixture. Smooth the surface with a flat straight pallet knife so that there is no residue on top of the mold, a plastic scraper could also be used.

When the lace is set, carefully peel it from the mold being careful not to break the lace, it is then ready to apply to your cake. Dampen the back of the lace with sugar glue or a thin layer of piping gel and apply carefully to the cake.

Note: Lace can be brushed with luster dusts or glitters, always make sure that these are edible. Food approved labels are often different in different states and countries.

# Stenciling

There are many beautiful stencil designs available in cake decorating and craft stores.

Stenciling gives the finished product a formal elegant look as the design is uniform and has clean defined lines.

It can be used as a way of enhancing the texture of a cake by using the same colored icing on the cake as the stencil work.

If a bolder design is required a deep color can be added to either the fondant or the royal icing to give definite contrast in colors which gives a very defined pattern. Black stenciling on a white cake is the perfect example.

## METHOD

1. Choose the desired stencil to decorate your pre-made cake and place on the fondant.
2. If stenciling on the side of a cake, tape can be used to hold it in place or have some one help to hold the stencil.
3. Royal icing should be soft enough to be easily spread over the stencil. If it is too runny the icing is susceptible to going under the stencil resulting in smudged, undefined lines. Freshly made royal icing will also help prevent smudging as it holds shape better when it is fresh.
4. Spread the royal icing with a pallet knife or scraper over the stencil, not too thick, with not too many stokes back and forth this will prevent the icing from being pushed underneath the stencil.
5. Peel back the stencil carefully from the fondant. The royal icing will crust quickly.
6. Patterns which need to be replicated close to the first part of the stenciled area will need to be dry before trying to apply the pattern to the next section.

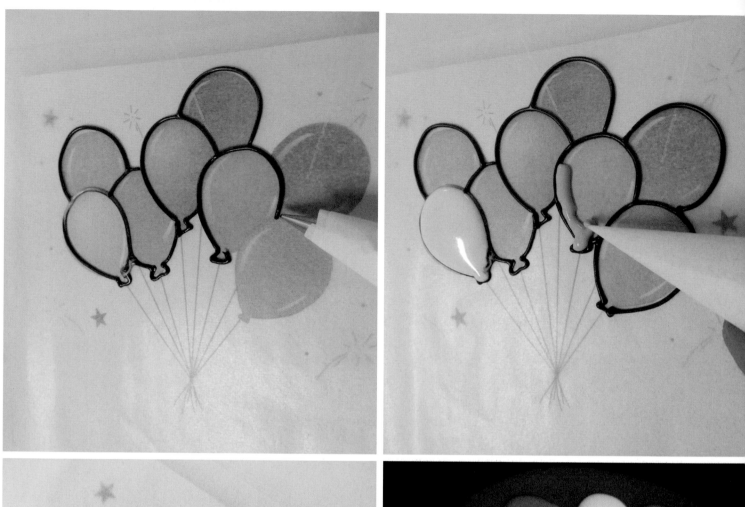

# Flood Work

Flood work is a very useful technique when making custom logos and designs or collars which look great when raised on top of a cake.

It is an old technique which can also be referred to as 'run in' work.

The trick to successful results using this method is to keep the design simple. Chose designs which have good clear outlines.

If the design has deep colors such as black, navy blue or red, a good tip is to do the dark parts first and let them dry before adding a lighter color next to it, this should prevent bleeding of colors.

## METHOD
1. Place a piece of waxed paper on top of a sturdy base board.
2. Slide the picture of choice underneath the greaseproof paper and secure with some sticky tape. Simple pictures with solid uncomplicated outlines work best.
3. Using royal icing and a number 2 icing tip, trace the outside border of the design. Pipe the lines inside which will divide the different colors.
4. Starting with the lightest color, mix some royal icing in a small bowl to the desired color then add enough water to the mix to make the icing runny. Add only a few drops at a time as the icing shouldn't be too thin.
5. Pipe the 'run in' icing inside the divided areas, repeat the process with different colors to define patterns.
6. Once all of the colors have been piped, leave to dry in a warm dry place. I like to leave mine near a heater to hasten the drying time which prevents colors from running.
7. Carefully peel off the backing paper. You can slide a knife between the paper and the icing to help ease it off if needed.

# Elegant Tea Set Wedding Cake

This beautiful cake looks stunning yet is quite achievable for a novice decorator.

The theme for the wedding was vintage lace using pretty pastels and tea sets from days gone by.

The table cloths were hand embroidered to compliment the vintage theme and jars full of old fashioned roses completed the elegant look.

The tea set on top is a miniature china tea set however a tea set made from fondant would look amazing on top of this cake.

The tiny flowers around the sides are simple cut out flowers which are easy to achieve yet look so pretty and elegant.

The lace around the cakes are made from cotton, but cake lace could also be used creating all edible decorations.

## METHOD

1. Bake cakes and prepare with ganache as previously described.
2. Cover the boards and ice cakes with RTR in pretty pastel colors.
3. Dowel the cakes with skewers or straws (this cake has small gaps between layers so cut skewers slightly higher than the top of the cake surface).
4. Place ribbon and lace around the base of all three cakes and adhere with a small amount of royal icing.
5. The flowers on the cake are simple cut out style flowers. Use cutters of your choice to make it original, and secure them to the sides of the cake using royal icing.
6. The top tier has small round cut outs with a few tiny flowers centered, the deep color in the center of the flowers is hand painted with food coloring.

Cakes

# Traditional Four Tiered White Cake with Roses

This traditional style wedding cake combines round and square shaped cakes to give a modern twist to the cake design.

The square cake at the base makes the ideal space for roses to be placed at every corner. The roses are a fantasy style rose which gives a full bloomed effect to the flower.

The techniques used to recreate this cake are:

- Quilting
- Hand made roses
- Piping

METHOD

1. Bake cakes and prepare with ganache as previously described.
2. Cover boards and ice cakes with RTR.
3. While the RTR is still soft, use a quilting impression tool to mark diamond shapes around two of the tiers.
4. Place the bottom tier on a base board using royal icing to secure.
5. Push straws down into the base cake, using royal icing between layers to secure, repeat this process for all four cakes.
6. Using a number 1 tip, pipe royal icing dots on the quilted part of the cake and push the silver balls onto the royal icing to secure them on the cake.
7. Place cake on a turntable and mark out even spaces with a tape measure, pipe dropped loops around the top of the other two tiers.
8. Make a selection of roses as previously described and secure to cake with royal icing. Ribbons can be inserted in between the roses with tweezers to fill in any gaps. Small filler flowers could also be used for this.

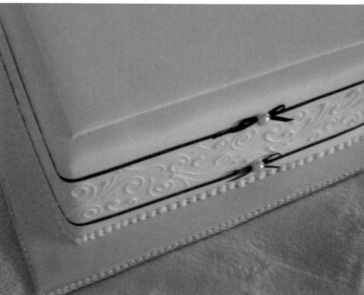

# Hand Piped Cakes

These beautiful hand piped cakes have the wow factor because of the steady hand and ability that it takes to pipe a design free-hand.

Practice is needed to gain confidence and expertise in order to be an expert piper.

A steady hand, even pressure and an eye for detail is the key to making lines and swirls blend together.

Have a pattern to suit the theme on paper to use as a guide, having it beside you while piping gives a good reference as to what swirls look good together and flow to make a continuous pattern around the whole cake.

Piping in black leaves no room for error so practice first on paler shades as any imperfections will be less visible.

## METHOD

1. Bake cakes and prepare with ganache as previously described.
2. Cover boards and ice cakes with RTR.
3. Stack cakes using tea straws for support.
4. Cut ribbon to go around the sides and secure with royal icing.
5. Use a number 1 piping tube in a piping bag with royal icing inside, pipe swirls, loops and curls on the side using smooth flowing movements.
6. A row of shell work can be piped at the base of each cake if ribbon is not going right to the bottom or beads and pearls can be placed at the base to give sparkle to the design.
7. Decorate with handmade roses or any ornament to suit the occasion.

# Celebration Cake
# with Flood Work Emblem

Flood work designs on top of a cake takes personalizing the decorations to a whole new level.

The design can be hand drawn onto a piece of paper to make a design that is unique.

Logos to represent a particular sporting club or organization can also be used as template to design a cake around the event that the cake will be used to celebrate with.

## METHOD

1. Bake cakes and prepare with ganache as previously described.
2. Cover the boards and ice the cake with RTR.
3. Choose a logo or picture of your choice and prepare as previously described in the flood work instructions. Once the emblem is dry (this will take a day or two) place on top of the cake and secure with royal icing.
4. The Thistles on this cake are hand made using gum paste. Start with a piece of green colored flower paste or fondant and hollow the center by pressing a pointed cell stick or ruffle tool in the top.
5. A small pair of curved scissors were used to make tiny cuts on the outside to give a spiky effect.
6. Use a thick purple cotton to make the stamens. Wrap the cotton around two fingers about 20 times, remove from your fingers and tie off the middle. Hook wire over the center and bend up the cotton so as that the ends are at the top, trim the strands to make them level and spread out to make them fluffy. Insert into the green gum paste.
7. Repeat for as many flowers as needed and arrange on the side of the cake.
8. Leaves were cut using a hand drawn template to achieve long pieces that are the height of the cake.
9. Script lettering cut outs were used to write the message on the board.

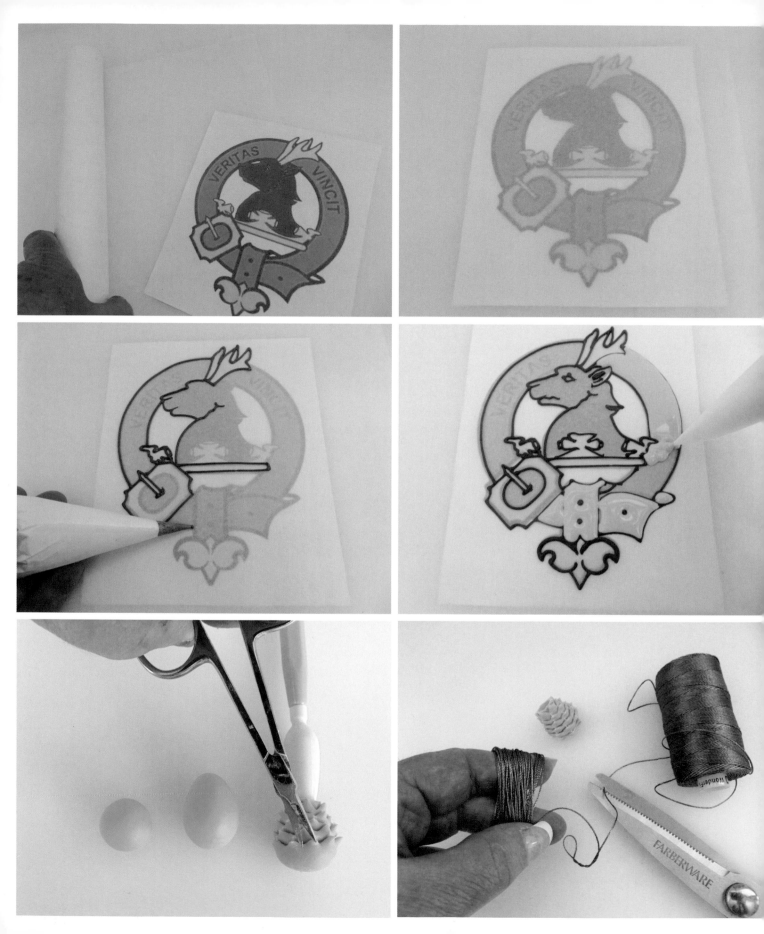

# Kitchen Tea Cake

This pastel green tea pot cake is soft and pretty and would look beautiful in any color to match the theme of the event.

The tea pot cake is made by using a round (ball) cake pan. There are two halves to the set, the cake is baked in two sections and joined together with ganache.

Round shapes are more difficult to cover with fondant as the icing tends to gather at the base of the cake.

To help prevent this from happening, make sure that you use a larger amount of fondant than required.

Having a wider area to off cut means that the icing which tends to gather around the base of the cake can gently be pulled out while the icing is smoothed with your hands to fit under with out puckering.

## METHOD

1.  Bake the cakes in a ball tin, on this occasion a square cake was used as a base but a round cake could be used instead.
2.  Prepare the base cake and the ball cake with ganache as previously described. Join the two sides of the ball together and wrap in plastic wrap. Place the cake back into the tin to retain the round shape and place in the fridge to set (about 10 minutes). Once the cake has set together, spread a thin layer of ganache all over the outside and place on a small board, leave to set.
3.  Cover both the round ball shaped cake and base cakes with RTR icing being careful to not get creases on the underside of the ball, trim off any excess and allow the RTR to firm.
4.  Make the handle and spout for the cake well in advance so that it is dry before inserting into the cake. Using RTR with tylose added to ensure that it sets hard, mold the spout thicker at one end with a bend in the middle and leave to dry, don't make it too big and heavy as it will be hard to keep it in place on the tea pot. Place some uncooked spaghetti sticks in the ends of the handle and spout to help keep it in place when inserting into the cake.
5.  Flowers and any other decorations such as the saucer and spoon can be made in advance using cutters, molds and gum paste. Follow the flower instructions as described previously.
6.  Place tea straws in the base cake, use royal icing to secure the tea pot (base board) to the bottom cake.
7.  Add all of the accessories to the cakes using royal icing. The handle and spout may need to be supported until they are set.

# Tyre Cakes

Black icing would have to be one of the hardest colors to achieve when covering cakes as tyres.

There are some good quality, ready colored RTR icing products available which takes the hard work out of kneading the icing when adding black food coloring to white RTR.

Airbrushing the final work is also a good way to achieve the depth of color. Even if an airbrush is being used make the base color of the fondant as black as possible to get the best coverage.

Treads on the tyres come in all sorts of patterns so no single technique is needed it is best to simply work with whatever items you have at hand.

For a thick chunky tyre such as a tractor, strips have been cut and placed angled on the black iced cake, this makes a tread that is bold.

For a car or bike tyre an impression tool is used. A straight frill cutter is used on these however making simple impressions with a scribing tool could be used.

## METHOD

1. To begin, bake a round cake to the required size, as per instructions.
2. Cover with ganache keeping the top edge of the cake slightly rounded to resemble a tyre.
3. Once the cake is iced, a tyre tread impression can be pushed into the icing, alternatively for a tractor style tread, strips of black icing can be rolled to 3 mm (0.1 in) thickness and cut to size.
4. Place interlocking pieces on the side of the cake securing with some sugar glue.
5. If making stacked tyres, prepare two cakes in the same way and stack as previously described in the stacking and doweling cakes section.
6. Make any extra embellishments to place on the cake such as racing flags, car figures, birthday messages or numbers etc.

# 3D Cakes

3D cakes have a real wow factor; the attention they get is well deserved as cakes that are carved into shapes takes time and expertize.

Once the groundwork has been done for the shaping of the cake, the basic icing principals remain the same.

TIPS FOR PREPARING:
- Keep it simple when cutting the basic shape, try not to create tiny spaces which are hard to get the icing into.
- Use a small paring knife to shape the cake, cut off small pieces at a time as it is easier to shave more cake off and harder to place it back on.
- It may be necessary to dowel parts of the cake together if the cake is particularly high.
- To ganache the outside of a cake which has been shaped leaving an uneven surface, wear disposable gloves and rub the ganache onto the cake with your hands to smooth.
- Cover the cake with RTR in the usual manner.

# Black and Gold Cake

Black and gold looks stunning together. The theme to the wedding was predominantly gold which made the black element in this beautiful wedding cake stand out.

Care needs to be taken when covering cakes with black icing as the cornflour (being white) can leave marks on the cake, which are hard to remove.

Similarly the gold edible powder, which has been painted on the lace and the sequins, can leave gold smudges, especially on the black base.

Note: To remove marks a small amount of rose spirit or alcohol can be dabbed onto the mark with a piece of kitchen paper, the alcohol initially leaves a shine but will dry if left for a few minutes.

The techniques used to achieve this very stunning cake are:

- Large peony roses
- Sequins
- Cake lace

## METHOD

1. Make three cakes to the size of your choice.
2. Follow the instructions on how to cover a cake.
3. Use the techniques previously described in detail to make the lace and the sequins.
4. Stack the cakes on top of each other using doweling or straws to support the tiers.
5. Ribbon or lace can be secured to the cake using royal icing, tie a bow to cover the joining ends of the ribbon.
6. Place the peonies on the cake, I like to place flowers so as that they are not symmetrically balanced as it gives a more interesting character to the overall design.

# Love Cake

This is a very simplistic cake visually, yet to make a simple cake which has very little detail look good, it must be iced perfectly.

A cake with clean lines, straight edges and no lumps or bumps is hard to achieve as even the slightest imperfection will be visible.

Pretty in green and pink it could be an engagement cake, christening or birthday.

## METHOD

1. Bake two cakes, I used a 23 cm (9 in) and a 15 cm (6 in) round cake pan.
2. Ice the cakes with ganache and cover with RTR as per previous instructions for covering a cake, I used green icing for the base and white for the top to match the theme.
3. Once the cakes are iced, roll some RTR (thinly) in a contrasting color and cut strips to go up the sides of the base cake. Secure these strips of icing with a small amount of water or sugar glue.
4. Using an oval cutter and lettering cutters design a message or initials to place on the front of the cake.
5. Finally place a hand made peony on the top to complete the look.

Dear Jacob,

You are to us a gift most precious that we will
be unconditionally grateful for and love forever.

Blessed be your baptism and future life.

**Sunday 17 May 2015**

# About the Author

Robyn King is a qualified pastry chef with 40 years' experience in the industry. She is a very experienced cake decorator and teacher of the craft and regularly does demonstrations at specific functions. Robyn belongs to cake decorating groups where she is able to not only share many years of knowledge but also learn new techniques and tips from other members.

In 2013 Robyn opened her own shop, The Embellished Cake Creations, supplying decorating equipment, baking products and running classes – whilst continuing to keep her hand in decorating wedding and special occasion cakes.

# Index

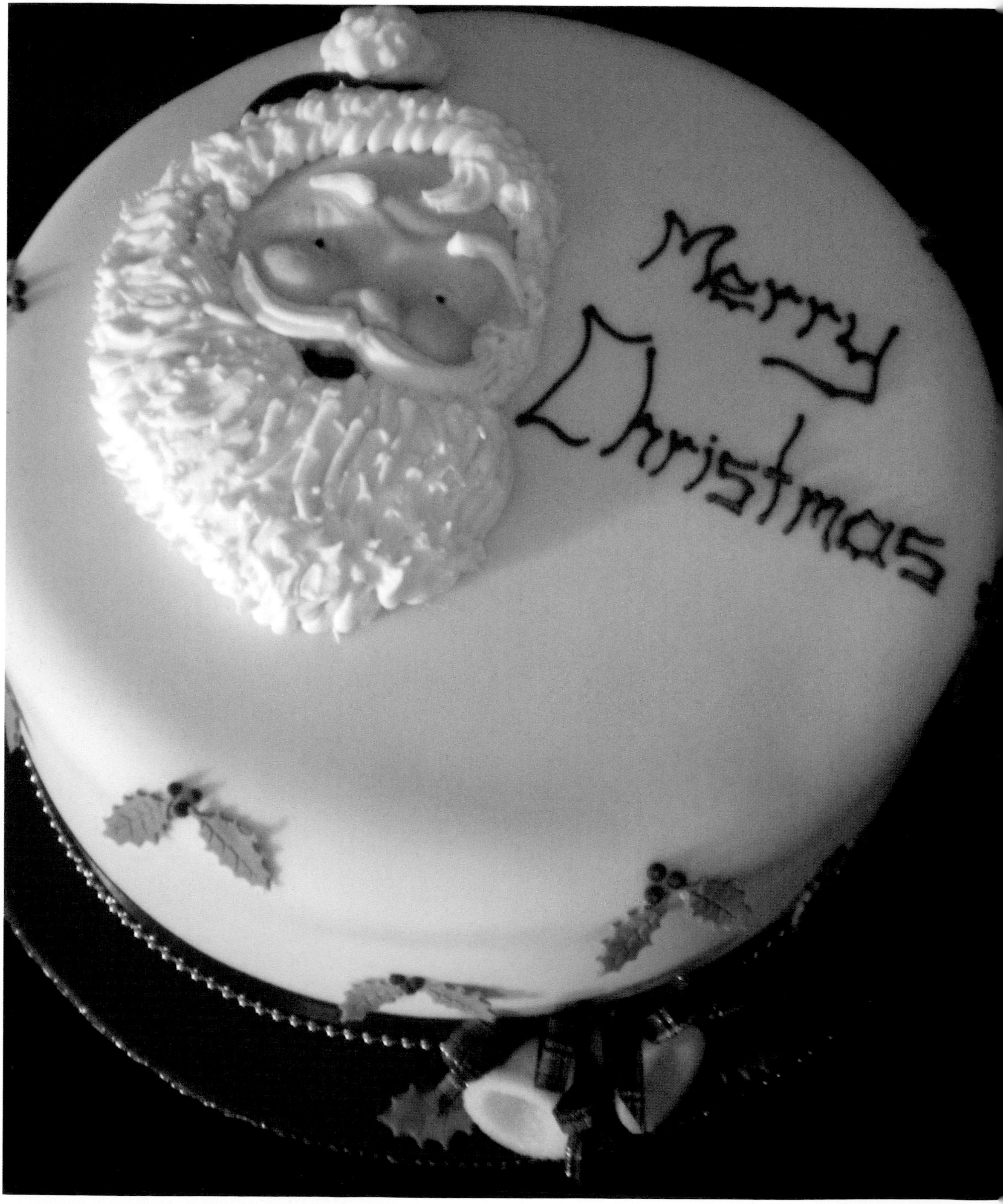
Merry Christmas

First published in 2016 by New Holland Publishers Pty Ltd
London • Sydney • Auckland

The Chandlery Unit 704, 50 Westminster Bridge Road, London SE1 7QY, United Kingdom
1/66 Gibbes Street, Chatswood, NSW 2067, Australia
5/39 Woodside Ave, Northcote, Auckland 0627, New Zealand

www.newhollandpublishers.com

ISBN 9781742577289

Managing Director: Fiona Schultz
Publisher: Diane Ward
Project Editor: Anna Brett
Designer: Lorena Susak
Production Director: Olga Dementiev

Printer: Toppan Leefung Printing Limited

10 9 8 7 6 5 4 3 2 1

Keep up with New Holland Publishers on Facebook
www.facebook.com/NewHollandPublishers